Guarantee Your Child's Success

David and Roxanne Swann

Mighty Seed Press
Clovis, New Mexico

Unless otherwise indicated, all scriptural quotations are from the *King James Version* of the Bible.

This book is specifically designed to help parents with children from infancy to adolescence.

Guarantee Your Child's Success
ISBN 0-9624589-0-2
Copyright © 1990 by
David and Roxanne Swann
P.O. Box 2107
Clovis, NM 88101

Published by
Mighty Seed Press
P.O. Box 2107
Clovis, NM 88101
(505) 762-7751
U.S.A.

Dedication

In dedication to these children whose obedience to God's commandments guarantees their happiness and success. "If ye know these things, happy are ye if ye do them" (John 13:17).

David Swann	J. Rashod Romeo	Natalie Barton
Janae Swann	Katrina Romeo	Allison Barton
Amanda Swann	Janae Crain	Reed Barton
Ginger Swann	Jeremy Crain	Vernell Mason
Jason Swann	Matthew Wall	Vernon Mason
Joy Swann	Trevor Wall	David Burke
Stormy Swann	Jennifer Southall	Ryan Gentry
Deborah Lowrey	Cheryl Southall	Joshua Tarver
Tabitha Chastain	Conrad Johnson	Andrea Sherrill
Jeffrey Chastain	Casey Johnson	Ann Nkeru
Leanna Haley	Andrea Johnson	Landon Tatum
Michael Haley	Allison Johnson	Misty Strickland
Jeffrey Haley	Stephanie Johnson	Robbie Darden
Michelle Haley	Spenser Johnson	Scott McCreery
Sasha Stiman	Jeannine Butler	Michael Fritz
Kristen Stiman	Stephen Monson	Caleb Spangler
Terry Alexander	Becky Patrick	Jennifer Jacoby
Tonya Power	Brett Patrick	Jose Matos
Joshua Power	Justin Taormina	Sarah Martin
Natalie Worthington	Andrew Taormina	Charles Pisaruk II
Stephanie Worthington	Danielle Taormina	The Children of
Antoinette Perea	Meyaka Williams	Odessa Christian
Amanda Perea	Marie Guillaume	Faith Center

Jeffrey Smoot	Leroan Graves	The Children of
Gregory Smoot	Latasha Graves	North Greenville
Bradley Smoot	Wesley Fish	Christian Fellowship
Letitia Lasiter	Lynda Fish	Larry Lasiter
Les Lasiter	Amber Salinas	Shane Salinas
Kristin Smith	Rowdy Strong	Tommy Smith
Kimberly Smith	Lana Collier	Joshua Stiman

Special thanks to the parents, grandparents, and friends of these children whose financial assistance has made this book a reality.

Also, we give a very special thanks to our wonderful parents, Terry and Shirley Swann and J. C. and Pat Stidham. Your continued love and encouragement propels us upward and onward to fulfill God's plan for our lives.

And, of course, to our three darling children, Janae, Jason, and Joy. . . you make it all worthwhile.

Contents

Author's Preface

In the everyday rat-race of laundry, cleaning, cooking, and playing taxi driver, it is so easy to lose sight of the purpose of raising children. With years now passing like months used to, it's not unusual to find yourself asking, "Is this what parenting is all about?" The Lord has a game plan for your home: for each one of your children to be a success. Our intent is to clarify what God has established as your responsibility, enabling you to get off the sidelines of frustration back into action.

With the target well fixed in your mind we'll arm you with the how to's of reaching your God-given task. Jesus said, "My yoke is easy and my burden is light." The Lord never designed stess and regret to steal the joy and fulfillment of raising children. You'll discover that the Bible way makes the burden easier and the future brighter.

David Swann

Chapter 1
Guarantee Your Child's Success

My wife, Roxanne, and I are often asked, "What stimulated a desire in you to teach parents how to raise well-behaved children?"

Our immediate response has always been, "We never planned in our wildest dreams that we'd ever write a book to help parents." When I proposed to Roxanne, we agreed to wait at least five years before having children. Less than a month after being united in marriage, we began pastoring our first church. Obviously, with so many new responsibilities, it made sense to wait those five years before embarking on any new adventures. I wanted to succeed at being a husband and a pastor. Both are quite a challenge in and of themselves.

Regardless of our forethought, within a few months we discovered that Roxanne was pregnant. You can imagine our surprise! (A better word would be shock.)

God Wasn't To Blame

Neither of us felt like this was *fair*. It was almost as if we were mad at God — as if it were His fault! But the Lord wasn't to blame; we were.

After a few months passed, reality set in, and we changed our attitude from dismay to anticipation! However, what we didn't know then that we know now, is that we were sowing rejection into our unborn child while she was being formed in her mother's womb.

Our words, attitudes, and feelings were affecting her

1

emotions. Even though our negative attitudes changed before Roxanne gave birth, the damage had been done.

The Fruit of Rejection

For months after Janae was born, she cried uncontrollably. We couldn't make her happy. We did everything we knew to make her comfortable, yet she wouldn't stop crying.

Have you ever gone to a restaurant to enjoy a relaxing meal, and before being served you are silently asked by everyone to leave? Wherever we went, Janae would start to cry, and we couldn't get her to stop. Our church nursery workers were relieved when services concluded, because Janae was such a problem.

One evening Roxanne taught a women's meeting at the church and I bravely volunteered to take care of Janae in her absence. Roxanne was only gone for two hours, but it seemed like an eternity. Before the night was over, I was ready to flush Janae down the toilet, singing, "I've been delivered, oh praise the Lord." I was frustrated! We were miserable!

Missing It As Parents

We knew from the scriptures that God said children are a blessing, yet we were not experiencing that promise. We knew that God hadn't lied about children, so we must be doing something wrong. We were missing it as parents.

There were times after work when Roxanne would meet me at the door with Janae because she needed to get away from the house and Janae for a few minutes.

We were desperate for help. We began to seek God for instruction. Our motive then wasn't to teach parents. That never crossed our minds! We sought God's help because our sanity was at stake! (I'm sure you've seen the bumper sticker that reads, "Insanity Is Hereditary — You Get It From Your Kids.")

We studied the scriptures with a compelling drive to survive. Thank God, the Bible does contain the answers we need as parents to raise pleasant children.

Like all parents, we had an image of how we wanted our children to behave. We wanted them to respect others' feelings and possessions. As pastors, we often visit our parishioners in their homes; therefore, we didn't want to call them ahead of time and warn them to put all their valuables on high ground so our "little blessings from the Lord" wouldn't destroy what they had worked so hard to obtain.

How Do Others See Your Children?

Young couples often inquire why others in the church don't invite them to their gatherings. The answer is simple: Their "little blessings from the Lord" are out of control, and no one wants their home destroyed!

Adults subconsciously reject disobedient children. What's sad is that it isn't the children's fault. Often the reason children suffer from a sense of low self-esteem is because they have been rejected by their peers as well as most authority figures.

In most cases, rejection begins with misbehavior. People don't enjoy being around disobedient children. Face it: Not one of us relishes the thought of spending an evening with brats.

Correct Discipline

He who spares the rod hates his son, but he who loves him is careful to discipline him.

Proverbs 13:24 *NIV*

Parents will eventually wish they'd never had children if those children aren't *correctly* disciplined. Proverbs 13:24 conveys they will even hate their son.

Our paramount reason for seeking God was that we wanted our child to be a blessing! We wanted to enjoy being parents, and we wanted Janae and any future children we would have to behave and be respectful. We'd seen in other children what we liked and disliked.

3

As Roxanne and I changed, we saw Janae change. Our church members noticed the gradual change in Janae until it became obvious that there was a distinction between her obedience and that of their children.

They asked us what we had done to cause such a transformation. It was then that we began communicating the things the Lord has so graciously revealed to us.

Our Heavenly Father Knows Best

Praise ye the Lord. Blessed is the man that feareth the Lord, that delighteth greatly in his commandments.

His seed shall be mighty upon earth: the generation of the upright shall be blessed.

Psalm 112:1,2

The first thing you must do to guarantee your child's success is believe that God knows best! He knows the best *way* to raise your children. All of His ways and commandments were given with our good in mind.

God is not egotistical, either. His attitude isn't like a child who says, "If you don't play with my toys like I want, I'll take my toys home and you won't get to play with them anymore." God is love. Every commandment from the Lord was issued with our best interests at heart:

And the Lord commanded us to do all these statutes, to fear the Lord our God, for our good always, that he might preserve us alive, as it is at this day.

Deuteronomy 6:24

So it is *for our good* that God put His will in command form. God didn't give us the "Ten Invitations"; He gave us the Ten Commandments.

If your children were playing in a busy intersection with cars zooming by at 65 mph, you wouldn't stick your head out the front door and *invite* your children to get out of the street. With all the emotion you could muster, you would in no uncertain terms *command* them to get out of the street! Why? Because you're egotistical and you like to flex your parental muscles? Heavens, no!

You command them because their life is in danger. The reason you demand obedience is because their life is at stake. You require obedience because you want to "preserve them alive." You do it because you love them!

Delighting in God's Commandments

These are the reasons God put His will and ways in a command form. The blessing that Psalm 112 describes will happen to us as we delight in God's commandments.

It's time the Church quit viewing God's ways incorrectly. Too often people think God is restricting them when He commands, "Thou shalt not commit adultery." Many interpret it this way: "Thou shalt not have any fun."

No — forever no — God knows that by rebelling against His command, we will experience inevitable death, just as surely as those children playing in the highway will eventually be run over if they don't heed their mother's voice.

The 18-wheelers of life called "sin" will run us into the ground if we don't obey God's voice. Change your attitude about God's commandments. Tell the Lord right now you're sorry for having a bad attitude about His commandments. Ask Him to give you *great* delight in His ways.

You must take greater delight in God's ways than in your ways — in the way you're raising your children, or in the way your parents raised you. You are destined to raise your offspring the same way your parents raised you if you don't get your mind renewed to God's Word.

Are you willing to change? Are you willing to raise your children in God's prescribed way? Are you willing to think and act on a much higher scale than ever before? Believe me, our heavenly Father knows best!

What Does God Want To Do With Your Children?

Correct thy son, and he shall give thee rest: yea, he shall give delight unto thy soul.

Proverbs 29:17

As I've stated, our greatest desire in seeking help from God concerning child-rearing was that Janae would be pleasant to be around. The above text promises that one's offspring "shall give thee rest." We *craved* rest.

Many nights Janae would cry herself to sleep. Many nights I wanted to cry *myself* to sleep! Janae was driving us crazy. At this point we couldn't even fathom that she might bring *delight* to our souls; we just wanted rest.

God Has a Better Plan for Our Child

Yet in the months and years ahead, as we pursued our desire to know God's ways in child-rearing, the Lord showed us His plan for our offspring. Our motive was simply an obedient, well-behaved child. God unveiled a much grander plan. His thoughts were much higher than ours.

He said in Psalm 112:2 that our seed would be mighty — powerful, dominant — upon earth. Notice the Bible didn't say they would be mighty when they got to heaven, but that they would be mighty right now on earth. We don't need to be mighty in heaven, for in heaven there will be no enemies to fight, no battles to win, no temptations to overcome. The Lord wants your child to be mighty here and now!

What man is he that feareth the Lord? him shall he teach in the way that he shall choose.

His soul shall dwell at ease; and his seed shall inherit the earth.

Psalm 25:12,13

Notice that this man fears and respects God. He respects God's ways and plan to the extent that he cooperates through obedience, and his seed will inherit the earth.

...I may cause those that love me to inherit substance....

Proverbs 8:21

The word "substance" literally means real estate. God has always been interested in having His people "possess the land." The Lord drove heathen nations out of the Promised Land so that His people could control it.

Throughout the history of mankind, God has repeatedly given possession of vast amounts of property to His people for His glory. If we own the land, we can exercise control over what happens there.

Prominent Children

For I the Lord love judgment, I hate robbery for burnt offering; and I will direct their work in truth, and I will make an everlasting covenant with them.

And their seed shall be known among the Gentiles, and their offspring among the people: all that see them shall acknowledge them, that they are the seed which the Lord hath blessed.

Isaiah 61:8,9

The prophet Isaiah is referring to people who love God and have chosen to serve Him. He said that our children — our seed — shall be known among the Gentiles. "The Gentiles" in the Old Testament referred to people who did not know God.

The Bible is saying that God wants to make our children prominent and known among peoples of the world who do not know Him. Verse 9 continues, "...all that see them shall acknowledge them, that they are the seed which the Lord hath blessed."

Can you imagine people acknowledging God's blessing upon your offspring? God wants His blessing so pronounced that even the ungodly will admit His existence and His active participation with men.

God wants to promote our children. He wants their

influence felt in the world. God wants our children to "infiltrate" every occupation known to man. He wants to work with their skills, enabling them to be the best school teacher, lawyer, politician, farmer, businessman, artist, musician, mother, father, grandparent, and so forth. All this is for His glory.

Biblical Examples

We have many Biblical and contemporary examples of men and women whose lives affected their generation as well as succeeding generations.

Joseph became the most successful agriculturalist and businessman of the known world. He had the entire world literally eating out of the palm of his hand during the widespread famine that took place in his time.

To this day, scientists in our high tech society are unable to duplicate Joseph's ability to store grain for seven years without its spoiling. God not only gave Joseph revelation about the future, but also secrets concerning scientific equations. God is the God of witty inventions; His secrets have not been exhausted! He has many ideas that will catapult your child into prominence for His glory.

The Bible records that King Abimelech said to Isaac, "Go from us; for thou art much mightier than we" (Genesis 26:16). It was clear to the Philistines and their king that God's blessing was upon Isaac (v. 12). They knew it was God's hand upon him that enabled him to become "mighty" upon the earth!

Children Who Know Their Authority

And this did she many days. But Paul, being grieved, turned and said to the spirit, I command thee in the name of Jesus Christ to come out of her. And he came out the same hour.

Acts 16:18

One afternoon Roxanne and Janae went grocery shopping at one of the local stores. It was Double Coupon Day, so the market was bustling with shoppers.

As Roxanne pushed her cart near the checkout stand, Janae said loudly, "You leave her alone, in the Name of Jesus!" The area got very quiet as everyone looked to see the little girl who had spoken so loudly.

Roxanne kept pushing her cart as if someone else's child had said it. When she was able to turn down a vacant aisle, she questioned Janae, "Why did you say that, honey?"

Janae replied innocently, "Mom, didn't you see that awful thing squeezing that woman's head?"

"No, I didn't, honey. What was it?"

Janae went on to explain that a demon had this woman in a headlock, and when she spoke to it to leave in Jesus' Name, it jumped off the woman's shoulder to the floor and ran out the front doors of the store.

Our Legacy: Our Arrows

As arrows are in the hand of a mighty man; so are children of the youth.

Psalm 127:4

Our children are a weapon against the enemies of God and man. As arrows are to a skillful archer, our children are to us against the darkness of this world.

In Ephesians 6:11, the Apostle Paul admonished us to put on the armor of God that would enable us to stand against the strategies of the devil:

Put on the whole armour of God, that ye may be able to stand against the wiles of the devil.

In all the armor Paul lists in this sixth chapter, we find only hand-to-hand weapons: a sword, a shield, a breastplate, and so forth. However, the Psalmist tells us about one weapon that leaves our personal life and sails far beyond where we now stand: an arrow.

In other words, we must point our children in an exact direction so that they may strike the devil and his regime long after we have departed from the earth. We must aim our "arrows" at targets that please God. God wants our children to be awesome spiritual giants for His glory! I pray that God expands your thoughts toward your children as He continues to broaden ours.

God's Twofold Guarantee for Our Children

Children, obey your parents in the Lord: for this is right.

Honour thy father and mother; which is the first commandment with promise;

That it may be well with thee, and thou mayest live long on the earth.

Ephesians 6:1-3

These verses are so familiar to most of us that we probably can quote them by memory, yet we haven't completely gleaned the richness of God's promise and plan for our children.

God said that He has a twofold promise or guarantee for children who obey His commandment. *God's first guarantee is that it will be well with our children.* Let's examine this promise for a moment.

What does it mean "to be well with thee"? Think of the possibilities. God wants it well with our children. He wants them to do well in school. I'm sure you want your children to make A's on their report card.

Janae had just started kindergarten when a young man asked her if she enjoyed going to school and if she was making straight A's. She said, "Oh yes, I love school, but I'm not making straight A's; just big A's and little a's."

Ten Times Wiser

The Bible says that King Nebuchadnezzar found Daniel and the three Hebrew children to be ten times wiser than the wisest of all the students of Babylon!

As for these four children, God gave them knowledge and skill in all learning and wisdom: and Daniel had understanding in all visions and dreams.

Now at the end of the days that the king had said he should bring them in, then the prince of the eunuchs brought them in before Nebuchadnezzar.

And the king communed with them; and among them all was found none like Daniel, Hananiah, Mishael, and Azariah: therefore stood they before the king.

And in all matters of wisdom and understanding, that the king inquired of them, he found them ten times better than all the magicians and astrologers that were in all his realm.

Daniel 1:17-20

What if your son's schoolteacher called and asked if she could have a conference with you? What would your reaction be? You'd probably think, "What has he done now? What kind of trouble is he in? What subject is he failing?"

The afternoon finally arrives, and you pull a chair up near Mrs. Smith's desk. She looks up over her reading glasses and leans toward you. Your hands are sweating, and your mouth is dry. You are anticipating the worst possible scenario.

Then you hear her ask, "What have you done to make your son so bright? Why, he's ten times smarter than all his classmates."

Wow! Wouldn't that be great?

When It's Well With Your Children

What does it mean "to be well with thee"? Your children will have an intimate relationship with Jesus Christ. They will be able to choose godly friends. They will be able to succeed at marriage. They will choose the right mate, and they will be committed and trustworthy. It means your children will be able to obtain and maintain a good job. They will be able to pay their bills.

If it is well with them, they will have a good, open relationship with you. They will want to spend time around you. They will look forward to holidays because of the special memories you've created through the years. They want their spouse and your grandchildren to experience what they relish.

God wants it to be well with them in every relationship and aspect of life. I don't mean there will never be problems and difficulties. As you well know, there will be many obstacles to overcome — many mistakes to be corrected — but through it all, *it will be well with them!*

Observe and hear all these words which I command thee, that it may go well with thee, and with thy children after thee for ever, when thou doest that which is good and right in the sight of the Lord thy God.

Deuteronomy 12:28

Overcoming Parental Fears

One summer as we traveled extensively throughout the country, I found myself with the subtle fear that someone was going to abduct Janae and sell her on the black market. It was during a time when missing children were prevalent in the news. I hadn't recognized this fear in myself at the time, but I was overly concerned when we were in public places.

When we returned home to Clovis, the yearly sidewalk sale was in progress and we, like all bargain hunters, went to "spy out the land."

After we'd been shopping for some time, we entered a men's shop and Janae asked if she could sit near a mannequin next to the entrance. We told her it was fine to sit there, but not to get up until we were ready to leave.

The store was full of shoppers. As we were about to walk out, a sports coat caught my attention, and I went to try it on. Janae thought we were leaving, so she got up and left, thinking we were right behind her.

A few minutes later, I decided against purchasing the

coat, and we walked toward the doors. Only a few minutes had passed. To our surprise Janae was not sitting anywhere near the mannequin. Thoughts began to race through my mind; images of someone kidnapping her seized my emotions.

In panic, I told Roxanne to look outside and I would stay inside and search for her. As I jogged through the store looking behind racks of clothes, all concern with what people thought about me left as I called her name.

These devilish words came: "You'll never see her again. They've kidnapped her."

I ran up the stairs and scanned the small room quickly. She wasn't there, and the feelings of desperation mounted. I felt helpless as the worst possible scenario kept replaying in my mind.

The Sweetest Question

As I ran down the steps, the sweetest question suddenly filled my heart and mind: "Would it be well with Janae if someone kidnapped her?"

As the Holy Spirit's words rang inside me, an incredible peace flooded my being. I said out loud, "Satan, you can't steal my daughter from me! I have a covenant with God. I have His guarantee on it. God said, 'Children, honor and obey your parents, and in doing so it will be well with thee.'"

I stopped running, and with a confident stride I walked outside, where I found Roxanne and Janae reunited. From that day forth, I've never feared for her life. God's Word tells us in Psalm 91:11 that He has given His angels charge over us to keep us in all our ways.

The Word of God can eradicate every fear from your life. Part of the curse that comes on people who don't obey God is that their life will hang in doubt, and they will fear night and day without any assurance (Deuteronomy 28:66). God's plan is to grant you specific guarantees that will produce peace in place of fear.

The Promise of a Long Life

The second assurance that His promises afford our children is that they will live a long life on earth. When we share these marvelous promises with people, invariably we're asked to explain why awful disasters such as childhood deaths take place in God-fearing homes.

I wish we knew. I wish we had more answers. Our intent is not to heap condemnation and guilt on parents. We grieve with any bereaved parents!

Let me state emphatically, "With long life will I satisfy him, and shew him my salvation" (Psalm 91:16). God's Word promises long life to those who obey God's commandments!

Guaranteeing Your Child's Success

Thou shalt keep therefore his statutes, and his commandments, which I command thee this day, that it may go well with thee, and with thy children after thee, and that thou mayest prolong thy days upon the earth, which the Lord thy God giveth thee....

Deuteronomy 4:40

In observing God's commandments, we can be confident that our days will be prolonged on the earth. If our children can be trained to obey God's Word as a lifestyle, then we've done our part in raising them to fear God and therefore guarantee their success.

The world's view of success is driving a BMW automobile and making a six-digit salary annually. Their motivation is position and prestige.

The kingdom of God, on the other hand, is built on servanthood. God's view of success is simple obedience to His will. When we comply with God's Word, we're a success.

Stop trying to keep up with the Joneses and get your eyes on eternal values. You can't take your cars or homes into eternity, but you *can* take your family! God's mandate to children is "obey your father and mother." In doing so, their days on the earth will be long.

It's so reassuring that cancer can't take my children from me. The AIDS virus won't kill my children. When I send my daughter off with her grandparents to South Carolina, I don't wonder if I'll ever see her again. She won't die in a car accident or plane crash.

Promises and Conditiions

How can I be so bold? I'm just saying what God has promised. This is what God wants to do for every child and every home. The problem has been that some have thought that these promises should automatically come to pass in their homes without understanding that each promise pivots on a condition. *The promise won't be fulfilled until the condition is met.*

In other words, we have our part to meet in this covenant, and God has His. We've tried to get God to do our part, and He can't. Therefore, the promise of Ephesians 6:3 stays on the pages of the Bible rather than in the life of a Christian home.

What is God willing to do for our children? The answer is found in the promises He's made. The question that must be answered next is: What does God want parents and children to do?

What Does God Want Us To Do?

In Isaiah 61:8, God was speaking through His prophet, telling us, "...I will direct their work in truth...." The Lord understands that raising children properly is a difficult job. He hasn't left us to figure out what we should or shouldn't do as parents. He declared that He would direct our work!

The Lord wants to work with us to raise a mighty seed on the earth. He will direct our work of parenthood "in truth." Jesus said, "thy word is truth" (John 17:17). The Lord is going to direct us in parenting through His written Word. If we are to raise a generation that God is seeking, we will accomplish it through regulating our responsibilities by His Word.

Our Contract With God

The Lord went on to say through His prophet, "I will make an everlasting covenant with them." "Covenant" is not a term that we use in our everyday lives. The word "contract" is a good description of "covenant."

If I were to contract with a cement contractor to pour a thousand feet of concrete six inches thick for such-and-such a price per running foot, the contractor wouldn't have any right to expect me to pay him in full if he hadn't completed the job.

Yet as Christians, we expect God to keep His promise even when we haven't fulfilled our end of the contract. In covenant, God has His responsibilities as defined in the contract, or Bible. We, as human beings, have our responsibilities as well.

Even the born-again experience has its own conditions: "That *if thou* shalt confess with thy mouth the Lord Jesus, and shalt believe in thine heart that God hath raised him from the dead, thou shalt be saved" (Romans 10:9). If... If.... If we believe in our heart and confess with our mouth, God is able to save us from sin and hell. Even though it is God's will to save everyone (1 Timothy 2:4), for His will to come to pass, we have to complete our job.

Our Children's Role

What must our children *do* before the Lord can cause it to be well with them and prolong their days on the earth?

Generally speaking, they must be trained to observe all of God's commandments (Deuteronomy 28:1,2). Yet before they can obey all His ordinances, it is imperative that they be trained to obey and honor you, their parents, as God's representatives. "Children obey your parents in the Lord (as His representatives)" is the way *The Amplified Bible* translates Ephesians 6:1.

The way your children respond to your authority indicates their respect for God. *You guarantee your child's obedience,* and God will guarantee your child's success.

The Old Testament Pattern

If a man have a stubborn and rebellious son, which will not obey the voice of his father, or the voice of his mother, and that, when they have chastened him, will not hearken unto them:

Then shall his father and his mother lay hold on him, and bring him out unto the elders of his city, and unto the gate of his place;

And they shall say unto the elders of his city, This our son is stubborn and rebellious, he will not obey our voice; he is a glutton, and a drunkard.

And all the men of his city shall stone him with stones, that he die: so shalt thou put evil away from among you; and all Israel shall hear, and fear.

Deuteronomy 21:18-21

Notice that "a stubborn and rebellious son" is one who will not obey the voice of his father or his mother. Your *voice* is what your children are to obey. If they don't obey your *voice*, they are disobedient. God places your authority over your children as the greatest authority in their lives on the earth.

You Are God's Voice to Your Children

You are God's voice to your small children. The way your child responds to your voice will determine the degree of his success.

According to verse 21, God called rebellion and disobedience to a parent's voice "evil." Too often we wink at our children's strong will and jokingly overlook their resistance to our voice. In Old Testament times, they would stone a young person to death for this type of repeated behavior.

In today's society, if you approached your city officials with your rebellious son or daughter, asking for help on how to change their attitudes, they'd probably scratch their heads and, with a blank look on their faces, say, "We have no idea, but when you figure it out, please inform us, because our kids are out of control, too."

In our society, it's unusual to find children who obey their parents the first time they're spoken to.

Wouldn't it be terrible if I visited your neighborhood and found no children playing outside? If I were to ask you, "Where are all the children, and what are those huge rock piles at the end of the block," you would sheepishly explain that the children had been stoned to death for disobedience.

Aren't you glad we live under grace and not under law? The truth of the matter is, if this were the accepted practice of dealing with rebellion today, you wouldn't be reading this book right now; you'd be under one of those rock piles!

The Disobedient Suffer a Prolonged Death

I really believe we live under a stricter covenant than those who lived under the law. Instead of putting our off-spring to death for their stubbornness, we sentence them to go through a prolonged form of death.

For example, they experience death in their relation-ships: in divorce, because they could never submit to one another; and in being fired from their jobs, because they wouldn't follow orders.

The Other Side of God's Promises

There is a "flip side" to Ephesians 6:1-3. If children don't honor and obey their parents, it *won't* be well with them, and they *won't* live a long life on the earth.

Your little "blessings from the Lord" must be trained to obey your voice the *first* time you speak to them in a *conversational tone* of voice.

The Bible says that having well-behaved children is a qualification for leaders in the church. According to First Timothy 3:4, "He must have a well-behaved family, with chil-dren who obey quickly and quietly" *(The Living Bible)*.

Even though this verse refers to ministers, I believe it should be every Christian's desire to have a well-behaved family.

Ideal Obedience: "Quickly, Quietly"

But what I want you to focus on is the *quality* of obedience the children display. The words "quickly and quietly" sound a great deal like "obey and honor." Obedience is an action. It is very obvious when children obey. They are to obey quickly when spoken to. Children often obey their mother the tenth time mama raises her voice to a screaming pitch.

In many homes, children don't even *notice* mama until the tone of her voice registers on the Richter scale! Why? Because children know your boundaries. They're smart. They've learned that you don't mean business until the veins on your neck are about to burst.

Why not train them to obey you the first time you speak to them in a conversational tone of voice? It's just as easy — and much less dangerous to your blood pressure!

The High Cost of the Bribe

Most parents use every type of manipulation available to get their children to obey, except the one that works. The most common is the bribe.

Mama tells her little blessing, "Now, son, we're going over to Sister Jones' house tonight for supper, and if you won't destroy the house, and if you'll be pleasant at the table, I will give you this Batman T-shirt." As your children grow, the bribes change, and usually they become more expensive.

And if you're not buying your children's obedience, you're threatening them to death: "If you do that *one more time*, I'm going to take you into the bedroom and beat your fanny off! You'll be on restrictions the rest of your life!"

When mama's eyes become bloodshot, her fangs grow, her fingernails shoot out, and she's screaming so loudly that she's spitting, they know it's serious.

But the Lord wants your children to obey your voice quickly and quietly. *Quietly* deals more with the child's attitude. We've all seen kids who did what their parents asked, but the whole time they were doing it, they were complaining. Gripe, gripe, gripe.

Obedience With Honor

Too often honor is absent from obedience. Your children may not say anything verbally, but their nonverbal communication is screaming loudly, "I can't wait until I get out of this house so I can do my own thing!"

It's like the little boy who was told by his teacher to sit in the corner with his face to the wall. He said, "I may be sitting down on the outside, but on the inside I'm really standing up!"

Just as there is a twofold *promise* in Ephesians 6, so is there a twofold *commandment:* Children are told to *obey* and *honor* their parents in the Lord.

I want you to understand clearly what our target is in child-rearing. It's imperative that we train our little ones from the beginning to obey our voice the *first* time we speak to them in a *conversational* tone of voice.

F. F. Bosworth said, "If you want what God wants for the same reason God wants it.., you become invincible." We know what God wants: honor and obedience to parental authority! But *why* does He want it?

Teaching Obedience to God's Voice

The Lord spoke to me and said, "If you'll train your children to obey your voice the first time you speak to them, they'll be prepared to obey my voice the first time I speak to them."

If we want to see an awesome generation, let's train our children correctly. There will be nothing impossible with our children if they hear God's voice and obey quickly! They will, without a doubt, be mighty upon the earth.

Daniel 11:32 promises, "...the people that do know their God shall be strong and do exploits."

How many times has God convicted you about an area in your life, dealing with you to stop doing something, or to start doing something else? Our Heavenly Father is the only parent justified in saying to us, "If I've told you once, I've told you a thousand times...."

The book of Proverbs is filled with such admonitions as: "My son, hear the instruction of thy father..." (Proverbs 1:8); and "Hear, ye children, the instruction of a father..." (Proverbs 4:1).

But we have trained a dull-of-hearing generation, because we have not demanded that our children value our words! God can't get through to them the way He would like to, because they have been trained not to listen. You'll never hear until you've developed listening skills. The God-ordained laboratory for this is the home.

Why the Prophet Samuel Succeeded

When the Old Testament prophet Samuel was a boy, he responded immediately to a voice he heard, even though the setting in which he obeyed — the Temple of the Lord — was unusual. It was late at night, and everyone was asleep. Samuel heard his name called (1 Samuel 3), and thought it was the High Priest, Eli, calling for him.

Most children today would have yelled back, "Don't you know what time it is? Whatever you want, get it yourself!" But Samuel got out of his bed and went quickly to Eli's side to ask what he needed. This explains why Samuel had such revelations from God: He'd been trained by his mother to heed and obey her voice.

God's Heartcry for the Home

The Lord spoke to me with tears in His eyes. (How did I know He was crying? How do you know when someone is crying over the telephone?) He said, "Son, I just want one generation that is raised from the cradle to obey my voice and do what is pleasing in my sight. Will you help parents to raise them the Bible way?"

This is why my wife and I wrote this book. We want to follow the cry of God's heart for the home:

> **Train up a child in the way he should go: and when he is old, he will not depart from it.**
>
> **Proverbs 22:6**

When do we start training our children to obey our voice?

The Hebrew word for "old" infers hair on the chin. This signifies that if we'll train our children correctly, when they get hair on their chin, they'll never depart.

The oldtimers used to say, "Don't worry about your teenage son who's into drugs, alcohol, or lust. Why, you've trained him right, and no matter how far into sin he gets, he has to come back, because that's what Proverbs 22:6 promises." But if we train our children Biblically, they'll *never* depart. They'll *never* go into sin.

"Hair on the chin" refers to puberty. When children leave childhood and enter into puberty, we call that adolescence. So we could quote Proverbs 22:6 this way: "Train up a *child* in the way he should go, and when he reaches adolescence he'll never depart from it."

The Crucial Years

The crucial years of training are from infancy to adolescence. This is because you must develop your child's respect for your authority, wisdom, and love during these years. Two-thirds of a child's lifetime impressions are established by age 5. Two-thirds of our child's lifetime knowledge will have been gained by age 7. A child learns more during his or her sixth year than a person graduating with a bachelor's degree learns from college.

Just because children aren't able to articulate the information they're learning doesn't mean they're not absorbing megabits of data!

However, even though I'm convinced that the years from infancy to puberty are the most vital years of training doesn't detract from the importance of the teen years. The teen years are, without question, the most important *teaching* years. The majority of life-altering decisions are made during these years. Yet most teenagers let dad's heartfelt instructions go in one ear and out the other. (I was amazed how smart my parents had become when I turned 21.)

It's Not Too Late To Reach Teenagers

Why won't teenagers heed your knowledge? Because they were never trained to value your thoughts, beliefs, and commands as a small child! If you are a parent of teenagers, don't get discouraged — get busy! You can redeem the time by repenting to God *and to your children* for your failure to raise them Biblically. You can do it! God will direct your work in truth!

Get hungry for God's help and His way of doing things. You'll have to humble yourself and stop doing things your way and choose His from now on!

Whatever untrained area you leave in your children, they will have to conquer through great struggle, or be conquered by it! It's like the old slogan for oil filters: "You'll either pay me now, or pay me later."

Just as it is easier for a child to learn a foreign language than it is for an adult, so it is easier for them to walk in the fruit of the Spirit and not fulfill the lusts of the flesh.

You can train your children to walk in love, not selfishness. You can train them to be self-disciplined instead of lazy; to be a completer rather than a quitter. How? Begin on their level, with their brothers and sisters. Train them to finish a page before they color the next page.

Teach them that God's Word is good because daddy's

word is good. God's promises are true because mama's promises are true!

A Godly Mother Touches the Centuries

John and Charles Wesley were great men of God who left their mark on the world. In fact, their influence is still being felt by people of all nations. John, after many years of ministry, wrote their mother a letter that contained the million-dollar question: How did you raise us? What exactly did you do that has made us so unswerving in our convictions? We see other ministers compromise their morals, and we so effortlessly serve God. Why?

Here is Suzanna Wesley's response to her son's question, as recorded in *The Heart of John Wesley's Journal:*

> I insist upon conquering the will of children betime, because this is the only strong and rational foundation of a religious education; without which both precept and example will be ineffectual. But when this is thoroughly done, then a child is capable of being governed by the reason and piety of its parents, till its own understanding comes to maturity, and the principles of religion have taken root in the mind. I cannot yet dismiss this subject. As self-will is the root of all sin and misery, so whatever cherishes this in children insures their after-wretchedness and irreligion; whatever checks and mortifies it promotes their future happiness and piety. This is that religion is nothing else than the doing the will of God, and not our own; that the one grand impediment to our temporal and eternal happiness being this self-will, no indulgences of it can be trivial, no denial unprofitable. Heaven or hell depends on this alone. So that the parent who studies to subdue it in his child, works together with God; any parent who indulges it does the devil's work, makes religion impractical, salvation unattainable; and does all that lies in him to damn his child, soul and body forever.

Mrs. Wesley strongly states that the one major character flaw that must be carefully removed from your child's life is self-will. As you train your children to obey your voice the first time you speak, you will have a clear picture of your child's self-will. It will surface with perfect precision. Self-will is noted in every person from infants to senior citizens.

Children who are trained to obey and honor our authority and wisdom will express self-will in many different forms, but we are not to worry, for through the help of God, we're going to conquer it before it conquers us! The delicate balance is to break their self-will without damaging their personality.

You're saying, "All right, I know what I need to do, but how do I get my children to obey me?"

Chapter 2
Encouragement, Praise, and Affection

I n this chapter we want to deal with three essential ingredients your child needs in order to be a success in life: *encouragement*, *praise*, and *affection*.

First, I define "encouragement" as *inspiring* your children to do something, *sharing* with your children your expectations of them in a given situation, *exhorting* them to obey; or the attitude or spirit by which you instruct them.

Second, "praise" is the response you give to your child after he or she has chosen to obey.

Third, "affection" is loving your children in word and in deed.

Paul said that our children would obey us if we would encourage them:

Children, obey your parents in all things: for this is well pleasing unto the Lord.

Fathers, provoke not your children to anger, lest they be discouraged.

Colossians 3:20,21

So if we're not to *dis*courage our children, then we're to *en*courage them. Another scripture that says much the same thing is Hebrews 10:24: "Let us consider one another to provoke unto love and to good works." Provoke means to "stir up a feeling."

27

It's our responsibility to "provoke" our children to love. I believe we need to "provoke" them to love God, to love us, and to love people everywhere. Stir up feelings inside of them to do good, to please you, and to please Jesus.

Motivating Your Child To Obey You

It's in the heart of every child to please his parents. Encouragement and praise will cause your child to want to please you. Encouragement and praise will "provoke" or stir up a feeling for your child to obey you.

Encouragement is letting children know what you want, and praise is the response you give them *afterwards*. Naturally, the response you give the child will vary according to his age.

We really "go wild" to show our children our praise and approval of them. They love to see us jump up and down, scream and shout, and dance around the room when they do something we approve of. It inspires them to do it again!

With our daughter, Janae, who is the oldest child, we can act a *little* milder. Gear your praise to the age of your child. Learn what represents praise and encouragement to that child, and then do it all the time!

The Importance of Encouragement

When Jason was two weeks old, my mama came from South Carolina for a visit and to help me get everything done.

I wanted Janae to be sooo good and sooo perfect that I jumped on her for every little mistake she made. But I wasn't getting the results I wanted. For the first few days Mama was with us, many things went wrong that shouldn't have gone wrong.

Finally, I went to my room and prayed, "Lord, I want to know what is wrong, because this is not how Janae normally acts, and I don't like her acting like this."

I wanted to *prove* to my mom that we'd been raising her granddaughter right, but I suspected she was thinking, "Bless these kids' hearts; they really need some help raising this child!"

When I stopped long enough to consider how Janae and I were acting, I saw that I wasn't provoking her to good works. I wasn't encouraging her. I was giving her absolutely no praise. I was continually on her case. My attitude toward her was very wrong.

Immediately, I said, "Lord, I'm sorry, and I'm changing." I saw that I wasn't fulfilling my role, so how could I expect Janae to fulfill hers? She wasn't accustomed to my acting that way, so she was acting squirrely. She was confused. She didn't know how to act.

But Janae changed immediately when I began to encourage her, when I let her know what I wanted her to do and when I wanted her to do it, and that I appreciated her obedience. It wasn't hard for *her* to act right when *I* was doing what I was supposed to do. In fact, it was easy for her then!

Let Your Child Be Himself

The first time we ever received an out-of-town invitation to teach on child training, I got so nervous, you'd have thought it was up to me and not up to God!

Every day for weeks and weeks, I drilled Janae, "Now, Janae, when we get to Little Rock, you've got to do this and this and this...."

The big weekend finally came. We stayed in the home of some friends. As we were all getting ready to walk out the door for the meeting, Janae started to cry.

I said, "Janae, what's wrong, honey? What's wrong?" I felt like blurting out, "Oh, do anything in the world, but don't get upset *now*. It's time for the meeting to start!" She just looked up at me and cried. She said, "Mama, I just don't know what you want me to do!"

I almost replied, "What do you *mean*? I've been telling you what to do for *days*. You *have* to know what to do!" But I knew that wasn't the right thing to say, so I didn't say it.

Then the Holy Spirit said to me, "If you'll just *encourage* her, she'll be all right."

Grownups Make Mistakes, Too

So I stopped and said, "Janae, I'm sorry."

You have to be big enough to let your kids know that you make mistakes, too. Children have an easy time following our example when they see us repent for our mistakes. Repent to your child and then pray right then and ask the Father to forgive you according to First John 1:9 — just the way you expect them to do! It's not important to be perfect, but be willing to admit error and make the necessary changes!

I got down on the floor with her, looked at her, and said, "Janae, honey, Mama's sorry." I said, "I've been so wrong to treat you the way I've treated you and to talk to you the way I have."

And I said, "Do you know what I want you to do this morning? I just want you to be Janae. That's *all* I'm asking; just be Janae."

She stopped crying and said, "Oh, that's easy." And she did extremely well.

I learned from this experience that we shouldn't place *demands* on our children when our attitude is wrong. We're supposed to *command* them in love — and that's encouragement.

Encouragement is causing others to believe that they can complete what you've instructed them to do! My attitude toward Janae was not positive at all. It was very negative. Even though I'd thoroughly instructed her on what she should and should not do, I was implying to her, "I'm so afraid you're *not* going to do right."

But when I said, "Janae, just be yourself — be sweet and kind and loving" — that was easy for her, because that is the way she really is. She didn't have to be someone she wasn't.

Encouragement Includes Potty Training!

We believe in using encouragement in all aspects of child training. We've encouraged our children in positive ways in everything they've learned — *including potty training!*

When we began to teach Janae to use the potty, I read many articles on the "how to's." Nothing I read seemed completely right. So, we went back to praise and encouragement. And it worked!

Four years later, here it is Jason's turn to learn. Again, I began to read up on the subject. Everything stressed how much harder it was to potty train little boys than girls. I thought, "Oh, no!"

So what did I do? Went right back to the same formula I'd used over and over again: praise and encouragement.

For many weeks when I knew Jason needed to "poop," I'd take his diaper off and run him to the potty. But then the big day came that off came the diaper and on with the underwear! I picked a day when the whole family was going to be home.

Many times, of course, I'd take Jason to the potty to pee-pee, and we'd all clap and tell him how smart he was.

Later in the day, I noticed Jason over in the corner by himself. I grabbed him up and took off to the bathroom, calling for Daddy and Janae. I sat Jason on the potty, with the three of us anxiously watching! His face turned red and with a couple of grunts, he did it!

This time, we all began to scream and shout for him. We were so happy! Janae sounded like a cheerleader, and Daddy did a cartwheel down the hall! Was Jason ever proud of himself! Immediately, he held tight to the potty again, face red, and wanted so badly to "please" us again!

Needless to say, Jason was potty trained that very day. To enjoy that kind of applause, why do something different? (He was potty trained for daytime, but not nights. We waited some time to do that.)

Some people will tell you that too much encouragement is bad for your child. That is not true! You cannot give your child too much encouragement and praise. Children thrive and survive on the encouragement and praise you give them.

Teaching Civilized Eating Habits

The same principles apply when training babies to eat properly. I'm not a sloppy person, and when I'd see little children learning how to eat, I'd think to myself, "I'd rather breastfeed my child for the rest of my life rather than go through that ordeal!"

I was with a friend once when she stated, "Well, it's time to feed little Johnny" She began undressing her baby. Then her husband took his shirt off, so I thought I had misunderstood, and they were going to give little Johnny a bath, not feed him.

But then they strapped the baby in his high chair, put his food in front of him, and food went *everywhere!* It was all over him, all over the floor, all over the high chair, and all over his parents. They probably prepared three times as much food as little Johnny actually needed, just to be sure Johnny didn't starve!

It was *awful!* I remember thinking, "Will I have to go through this when it's time to feed my children?" And I said to myself, "No, there's no way I'm going to go through that! There has to be a better way."

So from the very start, we'd say to our babies, "Okay, open your mouth *real wide.*" I reasoned that if a child's mouth gets open wide enough for the food to get *in,* he's not going to spit it *out!*

When Jason was still a baby, he ate very well. Every time he took a bite of food the right way, we'd say, "Oh, Jason, you've done so good! Oh, that's *so* good!" I'd clap and run around the kitchen with such pleasure! It took a while to feed him at first, but he soon learned that it was more fun to eat than to watch me!

Jason ate so well as a baby that people would often stop at our table in restaurants and comment, "I've never seen a boy this age eat this well in my life!"

Again, my husband and I used encouragement and praise to reach this point in Jason's training. We've "gone overboard" to let our children know how pleased we are with them when they do what we want. After all, that's what we adults live on, isn't it? We survive on encouragement and praise for ourselves, and so do our children!

Little Ones Can Answer the Phone

It may sound strange, funny, or even awful for pastors to admit this, but we *hate* to answer the telephone! When the phone rang in the evening, we'd look at each other and say, "It's probably for you. *You* get it." About the fifth ring, one of us would finally give in and answer it.

When Janae was barely three years old, we decided, "Hey, she speaks well enough — let's teach *her* to answer the telephone!" We thought this would not only be a good learning experience for her; it would also keep us from having to take turns!

So we taught Janae to answer the telephone. We rehearsed what she needed to say, and pointed out the things she needed to work on. The first time she ran to answer it, she had said, "Hello, this is Janae Swann" before she ever got the phone to her mouth! We taught her, "Wait until you get the phone to your ear before you begin to talk. Once your ear touches it, *then* you can begin to talk."

Janae answers the phone all the time now. It's amazing how well she does. She receives many compliments from people.

This experiment would never have turned out so well if I had quit after Janae's first attempt and said, "Forget it. She's too young. I knew she couldn't handle it." But we kept working with her and encouraging her.

In Proverbs 31 it says that a mother should give counsel

and instruction *with kindness*, for that's what encouragement is. Through encouragement and praise, Janae has learned a useful skill. And as we share additional pointers with her, we continue to give her encouragement. *Encouragement is simply instruction — given in the right spirit, with a positive attitude.*

We found that with the proper encouragement and praise, our children are capable of doing all kinds of things most people think they're too young to do.

How To Turn Defeat Into Victory

An example of this happened one summer, when we enrolled Janae in swimming lessons at the YMCA pool. Her instructor, while sweet, was not a godly person.

Because Dave was out of town during this time, I wasn't able to stay at the pool with Janae. There were things I had to take care of at the church, so I'd drop her off for class and pick her up afterwards.

On the last day of class, the children took a swimming test to see if they qualified for the next class. When I arrived, Janae's class was just finishing. She got out of the pool, looked at me, and announced, "I failed."

She was four years old, and that was the first time I'd ever heard those words come out of her mouth.

I was shocked and saddened. My first desperate thought was, "What do I do?" Janae had never failed in anything she had ever tried to do in her life! And I knew that the expression on my face was vitally important. I didn't dare look at her with a look that expressed, "What do you mean, you failed? You're my kid. You don't fail."

What I really felt like doing was crying for her, but she didn't need to see me cry, either! So I got down beside her and said, "Janae, you have not failed!"

She said, "I did, Mama. I failed."

And I said, "No, you have not failed, because we'll find out what you need to work on, and we'll keep working on it, and then we'll come back and you can take the test again."

Her countenance brightened. By the time her dad got home that afternoon, when he asked her how well she'd done on her swimming lessons, her response was, "There are some things you need to help me with and next time I'll do better."

She didn't say, "I failed." She said, "I will do better next time." *My response to her is what her response became to others.*

You Only Fail When You Quit

I went to her instructor and asked, "I need to know why Janae didn't pass her test and what I need to work with her on."

She replied, "Well, she had to swim five feet, and she couldn't do it."

The instructor had never worked with her on that skill in class. She explained, "The reason I didn't work with her is because I felt she was too young to do it. That was the first reason. Second, she's not old enough to go into the next class, so she may as well stay here."

For the next two weeks, Dave and I both worked with Janae and showed her the things she needed to know. At the end of these two weeks, the head lifeguard and instructor called me over and said, "Janae's doing so well with her swimming lessons." I told her the story of what had happened two weeks earlier.

She said, "Are you serious?"

I replied, Yes."

She said, "I'll pass her without her having to take the test again. She doesn't need to take a test from me. When she wants to go into the next class, she can."

The first instructor said Janae was too young to swim a distance of five feet. Two weeks later, she was jumping off a nine-foot diving board and swimming to the side of the pool unassisted.

Dr. Edwin Cole said, *"Champions are not those who never fail, but those who never quit."* Our children are not failures!

They just need parents who will love them enough to believe in them!

As one minister states, "I'm never down...I'm either up or getting up." You be the one with the outstretched hand to help them up! You be there for them!

Christian Children: Ten Times Smarter

Christian parents should believe for above-average results. After all, the Bible says that Daniel was ten times wiser than the wisest! Can you fathom reading a book on child development and saying to yourself, "My child is ten times smarter than this"?

It's essential that we do not place limitations on our children. Dave and I have discovered that our children can do many things that other children their age can't do! Why? *Because we don't put limitations on them.*

We decided, "Hey, if they *want to* do it, they *can* do it." And we've found that our children can do those things because we expect them to.

So when Jason decides he wants to do something, we encourage him and praise him until he gets it done. Different tasks take different amounts of time to accomplish, but we keep helping and encouraging our children until they accomplish what they set out to do.

Each goal accomplished gives them more confidence: "If I can do this, then I can do that." You can have the same results with your child, if you will encourage and praise him, let him know what you expect out of him, and let him know how pleased you are after he accomplishes his goal. Give him the approval and acceptance he needs.

Learning To Share

When our children are around their friends, we remind them that they are to be kind and pleasant, and to share with them. When they do this, we reward them with a great deal of praise.

The first few times Janae had to share her toys with her friends wasn't easy. She used to say, "Why do I have to share what *I* have? I had it first!"

A little boy was visiting her the first time I saw this happen. He took something away from her, and as he was taking it, she said, "That's okay. You can play with it." There were tears in her eyes, but she made that hurdle.

After the boy and his parents left, I said, "Janae, I was so proud of you when you did that. That was so sweet."

The little boy didn't even play with the toy. He didn't really want it; he only wanted it because she had it. In two minutes' time, he had laid it down and it was hers again.

How To Reward Your Children

The point is, God will reward our children if they will obey Him. But we as parents must be their rewarder here on earth. And the highest reward we can give our children is praise.

It's good to give presents, and children *need* presents sometimes. But don't *bribe* them with things; reward them with things. A bribe attempts to manipulate future behavior; a reward is a surprise that reinforces your pleasure with their behavior.

Proverbs 3:16 and 17 says that length of days is in wisdom's right hand, and in her left hand is riches and honor. "Her ways are ways of pleasantness, and all her paths are peace."

Therefore, you need to encourage and praise your children until you see them becoming pleasant and peaceful. The words a parent speaks are so important. A child can't possibly be pleasant or peaceful without hearing encouraging words from his parent.

Janae wasn't at peace that day in Little Rock because of the words I had spoken to her. Yet, when I spoke similar words, but out of a different attitude, that's when she became pleasant and peaceful.

The Damage Done by Disapproving Parents

Sadly, some parents never realize how important *approval* is to their children. Children who grow up without receiving their parents' approval *always feel a lack in their lives.*

For example, suppose a mother delegates a long list of chores to a child, but when the mother returns home after a hectic day at the office, she glances around the house and yells, "Why didn't you get such-and-such done?" — totally ignoring the fact that her child had worked so hard to accomplish the ninety-nine other chores on the list!

Such a lack of appreciation, especially over a long period of time, will probably make a child want to give up even trying, and may even lead to depression and significant loss of self-esteem in his or her life.

Bottled-Up Emotions

After my mother's visit to us when Jason was born, I broke down and cried and cried on the way home from the airport. At first Dave thought I was crying my usual good-bye tears because I would miss her so much until our next visit. But this time the tears were for a different reason: I was *so hurt* on the inside.

I said, "God, why can't my mother approve of me?"

She was there for a whole week, and we'd have nice talks every day in the living room. I just wanted her to look at me and say, "I love you, Roxanne." She always said "I love you" with her actions. During her visit, she bought special things for all four of us, but I wanted her to look at me and, for no reason in the world, say, "I love you," or "I approve of you."

Until that point, I had never heard her say, "You know, I think you made a wise decision in the husband you married, I think you're doing a good job raising your children. I'm proud of you," or "I approve of your living so far away."

Maybe I felt this so intensely because I was a new mother again. I don't know exactly what caused it, but all the emotions that were inside me spilled over.

I thought, "God, I need approval from my mother! I need to know that she loves me, accepts me, and approves of my life."

It's a two-hour trip home from the airport, and I cried all the way.

You see, as a young girl growing up, I always had such a desire to please my mom, and for her to be proud of me. Mama had worked all of my life, so it was the job of my four sisters and me to clean house. Mama would come home after we'd worked so hard and point out the things we'd missed.

I was an "A" student, seeking her approval. I strove to make good grades in school so she'd be proud of me. I made National Honor Society. Boy, was I proud. Surely, this would be it! But, even still, she never voiced to me how proud she was of me, or if she was at all. I didn't know.

Over and over, in different areas, I was searching for her approval. I never knew if I met her standards or not. On the inside, I always felt like I just wasn't quite good enough and couldn't do well enough for her to "brag" on me.

Dave and I had a long talk. I explained to him my feelings, and how many times I had sought Mama's approval but didn't receive it. He told me I had to forgive her! I didn't think I could. He helped me to pray a prayer of forgiveness.

Whether she ever changed or not could not depend on my forgiveness toward her. I needed to forgive her and I did.

After we got home, I sat down and wrote her a letter. I said, "Mama, you've been a wonderful mother in so many ways, but I *need* — I *have* to have — your approval. I've *got* to have it!" I was just honest with her.

My mother had been wonderful in so many ways. She established inside of me a love for God and a desire to serve Him with my whole heart. All my family and sisters and their families are committed and tremendous workers in the local church. Our moral standards are high. There's stability in our relationship with God and with our mates. All these things were imparted to us from our mom...but I needed her verbal approval, encouragement, and praise!

The Joy of Parental Approval

The day Mama got the letter, she called me and said, "Roxanne, I'm sorry. I had no idea I had been that way." She began to tell me on the phone, "You made such a wise decision, honey, in marrying Dave. Your daddy and I are so proud of you. We're so proud of your husband. We thank God that you're in Clovis. I wouldn't want you here unless it was God's will."

As we continued our conversation, Mama said, "Well, I thought you knew me better than that. I'm just that way and I guess I'll always be like that."

I said, "No! Mama, please! If you won't change for anyone else, please change just for me! God is love, and love would never be that way. Romans 5:5 says the love of God is shed abroad in your heart. God can help you change. God can help you love!"

"I can change," she responded. "I will change."

I felt as if I became a different person. From that very day, my life as a wife, as a mother, and as a minister changed for the better. I had a deposit made in me from my mama!

There is a very happy ending to this story. From the day she received my letter, my mom has completely changed. Today, my mom and I have a precious relationship together!

I love to go to my mailbox now and look for Mom's notes. Sometimes she works six days a week, but she'll still take the time to write me little notes that say, "I love you. I think you're wonderful." Or, "I'm praying for you today."

Sometimes during the week, Mom will call to say, "I just needed to talk to you. I love you, and I wanted to talk to you for a minute."

I love it! I love the transformation that has taken place in her because she made the decision, with the help of the Lord, to change! I love to freely look into her eyes now and say, "Mama, I love you."

In more recent years, I have found out that Mama was the way she was because she was raised that way.

You will treat your children the way you were treated unless you make a decision to change. Ask God to help you, and He will.

You see, I realized that here I was with my own family, living almost 1500 miles away from my parents, and I still needed my mama's approval. How much more do my dear little children need it from me now!

"You're the Greatest"

One Christmas, Dave and I conducted our child training seminar in my hometown. After we got back to the house, my daddy walked up to me, put his arms around me, and said, "I know I don't tell you enough, but I think you're wonderful. In fact," he said, "I think you're the greatest thing that ever was. You made a wise decision for a husband, and you've got beautiful children. And I'm proud to be your daddy."

My eyes filled with tears. I was proud to be his daughter!

Another time, we were scheduled to do a TV taping. When I talked to Mama the weekend before, I said, "Next week is when we do our taping. I just want to remind you to pray for me."

She said, "Well, I'll pray for you, but I know you'll do just fine." She knew we needed prayer, but she was also saying, "I trust you. I have confidence in you."

We've seen the opposite so many times when there would be a play or a program at school or at church. Why is it so easy for a mother to walk up to someone else's child and say, "Oh, you were so cute; you did so well," and turn to her own child and say, "We went over that material so many times! How on earth did you mess it up?"

Perhaps you go to coffee after the performance, and everyone's praising your child, and you say, "Well, if you knew what Susie was *supposed* to have done, you'd know she really didn't do well at all." And there your child sits, hearing you!

Words of Approval Are Eternal

I believe with all my heart that parents desire to respond positively. Don't let anything keep back words of approval.

Our children *have* to have our encouragement and praise. They *survive* on the love and encouragement they receive from us as parents!

The little girl who got the praise from another mother probably could have cared less, although it felt good for a minute. That statement wasn't eternal to her, because it didn't come from her own mother. *Your words to your child are eternal words that Proverbs 6 says will talk to them everywhere they go.*

My son, keep thy father's commandment, and forsake not the law of thy mother:

Bind them continually upon thine heart, and tie them about thy neck.

When thou goest, it shall lead thee; when thou sleepest, it shall keep thee; and when thou awakest, it shall talk with thee.

For the commandment is a lamp; and the law is light; and reproofs of instruction are the way of life.

Proverbs 6:20-23

I don't want negative words from my lips following my children everywhere they go in life, telling them, "We worked on it, but you didn't do it right. You didn't do good enough. You *can't* make it."

Inspire Them With the Word

Your words, whether positive or negative, will follow your children into other situations and circumstances in life. They are the only words your children know. They determine your children's self-image and self-worth. If your words are negative, they will echo in your child's heart, and he will hear, "My mom doesn't think I can do it."

We have trained our children to resist every time a thought comes to them that "I can't do this." We say, "Honey, Philippians 4:13 says you can. You can do all things through Christ Jesus. He will help you. He will strengthen you. He will cause you to be able to do what you need to do."

You see, for every situation that comes up in their life, we feed them the Word. When they say, "I'm afraid," we say, "No, God hasn't given you a spirit of fear, but of power and of love and a sound mind. You resist the devil in the Name of Jesus, and he has to flee from you."

We're always working godly principles into them through encouragement and praise. When they do resist the devil, he leaves them, and we say, "Glory be to God, you *can* do it! The devil's not just afraid of Jesus and us; he's afraid of you, too!"

Our words are very important to our children. We are speaking words that will keep them, guard them, and lead them in life. By speaking the right words to them, we are building the proper self-esteem into them, so they will think highly of themselves, and believe in themselves.

Guard Your Long-Range Goals

A psychologist said, "Never sacrifice the long-range goal of a good self-image for the present satisfaction of a high-quality performance."

We may be tempted to speak harsh words today to correct something in our child's life, losing sight of our future goals for this child. Be careful if you are a perfectionist that you don't wait for top performances before you acknowledge your child's accomplishments.

Don't you want your child to turn out to be someone who thinks properly and has high self-esteem and strong character?

For example, I didn't scold Janae because she didn't pass her swimming test the first time. If I had, she might have thought she *couldn't* succeed every time she got in the water afterwards.

In other words, I didn't sacrifice my long-range goals for her life just because she seemingly failed a test in the eyes of man.

I Think You're Wonderful!

"More children are abused with *words* than in their physical bodies," a psychiatrist once wrote. He stated that it is much easier for children to get over *physical* abuse than *mental* abuse, even though it takes a long time. He said, "Most children never get over abuse caused by the words of their parents."

This is another reason why you *must* watch your words. Set a guard over your mouth when you speak to your children! Don't speak any words to your child that you wouldn't speak to a dear friend.

My husband and I have *learned* to do this with other people. We have placed a guard over our mouths concerning what we say and how we act toward others. You probably have, too. But have you thought of doing it when dealing with your children?

You may argue, "But home is home, and that's who I am."

You need to change who you are at home, then, and *be who you are outside the home,* so you can speak encouraging, helpful, and loving words to your children. And don't compare your children; it will cause strife between them.

Inspire them. Encourage them in who they are. Children

need to know they're good. They need to believe that their mom and dad think they're the greatest thing in the world. Let them know that you think they're *wonderful*. And don't put limitations on them: Teach them they can do *anything!*

Each child is unique in himself. Build on the uniqueness of that child. Every child should know that he is special, made in the image of God, and the only one of his kind.

Teaching Children To Love People

Loving your children will enable them to be lovers. First John 4:19 says, "We love him, because he first loved us." We could not have loved God had He not loved us first.

One day Janae and I were in the grocery store. Since she was too big to sit in the child carrier on the grocery cart, she was sitting on the rack underneath.

I parked the grocery cart in the produce area, got the items I needed, and started off again, but the cart seemed a lot heavier than before. It was so full, I couldn't see the bottom. I kept thinking, "Surely I didn't get *this* much stuff," but I was preoccupied with my grocery list. Halfway down the next aisle I heard little girls giggling.

I stepped back and said, "Janae..." Another little girl peeked out at me. I said, "Honey, who are you?" She told me her name, and Janae said, "It's all right, Mom. She looked lonely, so I told her to come ride with us." The little girl thought it was wonderful, but we had to go find her daddy.

This happened because we've loved Janae so much, it's natural for her to love other people. It's natural for her to show affection to other people. She doesn't have a problem loving other people, because we've loved her.

In the beginning, Jason was not the "loving" child we wanted him to be. But the Bible says, "They'll know we are Christians by our love." So we would all love on Jason, even when he didn't like it!

When he was about 3 years old, one night he came into the bedroom and woke me up. He whispered, "Shh... Scoot over and let me in." Of course, I told him no, that he needed to go back and get into his own bed.

"But Mama," he whispered, "you don't understand. I need some snuggles. I need *your* snuggles!" How could I resist? I scooted over and he climbed in for some hugs and kisses! He loves us...because we first loved him. We've made Jason a lover!

Teaching Children To Trust God

David said in Psalm 22:9 that he learned to trust in God at his mother's breast. That's closeness. That's affection. So the closeness and affection we show our children will cause them to be able to trust in God. It will instill a trust in them for their heavenly Father.

Moms and dads, I don't care how old your children are: It's important for you to hold them, caress them, and show them affection, whether they are a boy or a girl.

The world has tried to pervert our minds with the idea that fathers can't show love and affection to their sons. They warn, "You're going to create a weird son if you show him affection, men." The opposite is true!

The reason why men reach out to other men in homosexual relationships is because they need a man's love. And that's the reason why women reach out to another woman in lesbian relationships: They need the affection and approval of another woman.

Parents, that's why God put us here: We're to show our children the godly love and affection they need. They *have* to have it from us.

When we first started teaching on child training, we didn't teach this aspect at all, and people were not getting results from our teachings.

One day my mother-in-law called, and I asked her to pray for us. I said, "We don't know what we're doing wrong." In two days she called back and said, "I know what it is."

I said, "What?"

She said, "You've never taught on how you pour your life, your love, and your affection into Janae."

As we began to look around us, we saw that there are many parents who don't know how to love their children.

Affection: A Critical Ingredient

I sit and rock with my children and we read books together. I hold them. I love them. If they went a day without getting love, hugs, and kisses from their parents, they would think that the world had come to an end.

Affection is critical to your children's development. Psalm 36:7 says, "How excellent [or how precious] is thy lovingkindness, O God! therefore the children of men put their trust under the shadow of thy wings."

Love will instill security, confidence, and trust into your children's character. It will make them lovers of people. It will cause them to be secure.

Children need *affection*, *touching*, and *holding* from their parents.

The Importance of the Human Touch

A hospital in Albuquerque was having a problem with premature babies dying. Then they found that the parents of these critically ill babies often were not available to visit them. So they started hiring mothers to come and hold the children when the parents were not able to be there. Since then, they have seen a tremendous recovery rate among these infants.

Why? *Because children survive on the love and affection that they receive from their parents.*

How do we show affection to our children?

The number one way is to tell them! Tell them every day, several times a day, "I love you."

Let them hear you say:

"You're special to me."

"You are so sweet and so kind and so pleasant."

"I'm proud of you for being such a good boy."

"I'm so glad you're a part of our family."

"I'm proud to be your Mom."

"I'm proud to be your Dad."

Pack special love notes in their lunch box, or in their suitcases when they're spending the night away from home.

Spend time with them doing things they enjoy:

Go on walks together.

Read books to them.

Play games with them.

Let them choose what they would like to do! Find out what's fun for them!

We enjoy spending time with each of our children individually. Janae loves for her daddy to take her on "dates"! Just the two of them will go out and eat together and do something fun.

What memories! You'll both treasure them forever!

Give yourself to your children. Spend some time with your children every day. Engage in conversation with them. Learn to listen to and enjoy them.

The way in which an infants' needs are met often has a great deal to do with their response to people and situations throughout their lives.

Some of you may say, "But I don't have an infant anymore. My children are already grown." You can still make up time. You *can*. The grace of God will allow you the make up time that you need. We have seen older children change.

Ephesians 5:2 *(New International Version)* tells us to live a life of love. Psalm 32:8 says, "I will instruct thee and teach thee in the way which thou shalt go: I will guide thee with mine eye."

Our eyes should not be eyes of sadness, gloom, and "I'm

going to get you." We should be able to instruct and guide our children with the eyes of love, compassion, tenderness, and affection.

What Real Love Does

Love isn't real love if it doesn't encourage and praise. Love is always an encourager and praiser.

Thou shalt love the Lord thy God with all thine heart, and with all thy soul, and with all thy might.

And these words, which I command thee this day, shall be in thine heart:

And THOU shalt teach them diligently unto thy children, and shalt talk of them when thou sittest in thine house, and when thou walkest in the way, and when thou liest down, and when thou risest up.

Deuteronomy 6:5-7

Notice there are *no breaks* in the training of children. You are to teach your children to love every moment of every day. But first love has to be in the parents' heart. This scripture said, "These words which I command you, that are in your heart, are the words that you are to command your children."

The Greatest Gift Is Love

The greatest thing that you can give your children is love, because love encompasses the whole spectrum of life.

I once read a slogan that said, "The greatest thing you can give your child is not time, but you." Don't begrudge the time you need to spend with your children and the things they desire out of you. Go overboard with your encouragement, praise, and affection.

Some parents will argue, "Don't you believe that I can spoil my child by loving him too much?" Children are spoiled by allowing them to have their own way, not by giving them too much love!

Jesus Christ gave His life for us. It didn't spoil us. We

can't spoil our children by holding them and letting them know the love that's inside us for them.

No, it won't spoil them. Instead, it will cause them to excel and do things most men think are impossible!

Chapter 3
The Art of Discipline

He who spares the rod hates his son, but he who loves him is careful to discipline him.

Proverbs 13:24 *NIV*

L ove must be the outstanding motive for discipline. Love is the foundation for all of our training. When we think of love, we instinctively picture *acceptance, affection,* and *approval.* I've entitled this "AAA treatment." Every person desires "triple-A treatment."

One hotel chain in our nation has this service motto: "Aggressive Hospitality." The reason I've given them repeat business is because their employees exemplify this motto.

The Craving for Acceptance

The basic emotional need of every human being is to be accepted. We've all seen how peer pressure exerts its influence in teenagers. Most students don't skip school by themselves. It's because they're desperate for acceptance, so they go along with the crowd.

When they drink alcohol and get drunk, it's usually with others. They experiment with drugs because friends offer them drugs with the underlying attitude, "You're not cool if you don't do this." People do not enjoy being alienated by those whom they esteem. We repel rejection and gravitate toward those who accept us.

After looking closely at some of the recent teen suicide

statistics in our nation, we see this glaring reality staring us in the face.

One young man was senior class president in his high school. He was popular with his classmates and a favorite with his teachers. Yet all this notoriety didn't make him happy. *Popularity* is when others feel good about you, but *happiness* is when you feel good about yourself. This young man had the acceptance and approval of everyone but his parents. So he committed suicide.

"AAA Treatment" for Children

Mom and Dad, your children need "AAA treatment." I'm convinced that if your children receive an abundance of approval from you, when their peers tempt them to disregard the values you've instilled in them, they'd rather have your acceptance than their classmates'.

One of the meanings of the word "train" is "to develop an appetite for what is good." Our children will develop a taste for what is good and right not only as we instruct them, but as we approve and praise them when they respond as we've taught them to.

Get emotional! Get excited about their obedience! Make a "big deal" out of their accomplishments. Convey your approval both verbally and physically. Give them a "high five," a "low five." Be your children's biggest fan. Be their loudest cheerleader.

While attending Bible school, I officiated at sporting events to supplement my income. Often, I'd find myself watching child-parent relations unfold during a game. One such example happened during the last two minutes of the Little League's championship football game. The team that was losing had moved the football down to within 10 yards of the go-ahead touchdown.

The quarterback dropped back to throw a pass. As he stopped scrambling and set up to throw, the horn sounded to end the game. He saw what he thought was a wide open receiver in the end zone. Just as the ball was about to reach his teammate, a defender stepped in front of the receiver and intercepted the pass to prevent the win.

The coach and all the players swarmed the boy who won the game for them. Other parents came on the field and patted him on the back.

After all the dust cleared — after his teammates and their parents had congratulated him — there stood his dad. What an opportunity for this father to affirm his pleasure! This was the perfect time to show his pride for his son.

Instead, the Dad said, "You're lucky! You covered the wrong man. If that quarterback had seen your man on the other side of the field, your team would have lost! I can't believe you got so lucky."

What a jerk! I wanted to take the man, tie him to a post, and beat some sense into him. This was neither the time nor the place to correct his son. The boy was a hero to everyone but his own father! If that father doesn't change, his son will grow up and have nothing to do with him. Everything he stands for, his son will be against.

Children *crave* "AAA treatment." If this boy received the approval he so desperately needed from his parents, there would be no limit to what he could accomplish in life. The cycle of love begins with "AAA treatment."

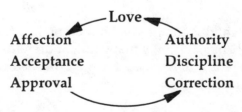

If you want your children to make A's on the report card of life, then add one more "A" to the "AAA treatment." That "A" stands for authority. *Children must be trained to submit to authority.*

Submission to Authority Must Be Taught

As a society, we are self-willed. We want what pleases us, not what benefits everyone else. The most common reason workers are fired from their jobs is because they wouldn't submit to their boss. Marriages crumble because husbands won't accept responsibility, and wives won't submit to their husband's authority.

Yet submission to authority should be a way of life. Everything would be in utter confusion if rules weren't followed. Think what it would be like if no one respected our traffic laws! How would you like it if people drove in the wrong lane, or refused to stop at stop signs or red lights? We would have a lot of wrecks!

That is *exactly* what rebellious people are experiencing every day in their lives. They have not respected authority; therefore, "wrecks" are occurring in their lives at an alarming rate. For example, divorce is at an all-time high. Bankruptcy is more common than ever before. Our national and personal debts are soaring, creating enormous stress nationally and individually.

We must return to the basic fundamentals of life. It is imperative that these fundamentals be ingrained into our offspring.

A wise son...is the fruit of his father's instruction and correction....

Proverbs 13:1 *Amp.*

Every child is the product of parental instruction and correction. Thus, it is vital that your children learn early in life that there is a *consequence* for their disobedience, and a *reward* for their obedience.

The Consequences of Sin

Often people continue in sin because they seem to experience no meaningful consequence that convinces them to cease. The Bible calls sin "deceitful." It is deceptive because sin doesn't destroy you overnight.

Romans 6:23 says, "the wages of sin is death." One day as you're minding your own business, you hear a knock on the door of your life. You answer the door and, to your surprise, there stands the master of sin, Satan.

You ask, "What do you want?"

He responds by smiling and saying, "You've served sin faithfully, and I've brought you your wages." He then proceeds to pay you with death: death in your relationships, death in your job, death in your marriage, death in your mental and emotional health, death in your physical health, and death in your spiritual life. Sin is no friend to you!

Sin is deceitful because you think you're getting away with it without suffering any negative consequences. However, Numbers 32:23 says, "...be sure your sin will find you out." Sin is like a boomerang: It may leave your life, but it will always come back to haunt you.

This is partly how they develop that taste for what is good. The other way is being rewarded for *every* obedience. Children need to be trained through repetition that disobedience to God's will brings an undesirable consequence!

Teach the Rewards of Godly Behavior

Hebrews 11:6 says, "God...is a *rewarder* of them that diligently seek him." It is godly to reward your children. Approval is the highest form of reward you can share with your children when it is done with sincerity and excitement. If you're not excited, it won't turn them on.

Be hyper! Be crazy! Be emotional! They'll esteem obedience because you think it's so great when they obey!

Special privileges are tremendous rewards. (It's not a privilege if it's commonplace.) When your children are obedient, tell them, "You get to stay up," or, "You get to be out later because you've been sooo obedient" — and then name some area where they've been obedient. The more *specific* you are concerning their actions or attitudes that please you, the more effective the reward will be to them.

Buy gifts that bless them, and as they open these gifts, tell them you enjoy buying them things because you appreciate this or that. (Children are like a piece of property in one way: They will appreciate in value if you do your part in taking care of them!)

When taking your family on vacation or other "fun things," remind them of your pleasure with their obedience. A genuine "thank you" can go a long way when it is accompanied by something they enjoy. If you enjoy doing things with your children now, when they're young, they'll enjoy doing things with you when they're older.

One pastor told Roxanne and me that his college-aged son asked if he and his date could spend the evening with them. Of course the father was elated that his son would want to "hang out" with them.

Children are the culmination of Dad and Mom's instruction and correction (Proverbs 13:1 *Amplified*). Children need to learn the consequence of disobedience under your loving, gentle control, rather than in the world's cruel setting of "performance or else." And you know the "or else" is rejection. In the world you either perform, or you are fired. The world won't be concerned with your child's well-being; just his or her output.

Discipline Motivated by Love

In the January 1986 issue of *The Reader's Digest,* a writer gave the statistics that 83 percent of American parents spank their children — yet only 40 percent of this group believes it does any good.

I was surprised that so many do spank, yet so few are seeing any tangible results. As we saw earlier, Proverbs 13:24 *(NIV)* explains this failure:

> He who spares the rod hates his son, but he who loves him is careful to discipline him.

The two words that spotlight our answer for such a high degree of failure are "careful" and "love." If our discipline is motivated by love, we'll be careful how we administer the rod as well as where, when, why, around whom, and in what attitude.

You are destined to discipline your children like your parents corrected you unless your mind gets renewed to God's original plan, which is found in His Word.

What does the Bible say we're to use to discipline our children? We already saw the answer in Proverbs 13:24: the rod. Now let's look at these additional scriptures:

> **Foolishness is bound in the heart of a child; but THE ROD of correction shall drive it far from him.**
>
> **Proverbs 22:15 *KJV***

> **THE ROD and reproof give wisdom: but a child left to himself bringeth his mother to shame.**
>
> **Proverbs 29:15 *KJV***

> **Withhold not discipline from the child, for if you strike and punish him with the rod, he will not die.**
>
> **You shall whip him with THE ROD And deliver his life from Sheol.**
>
> **Proverbs 23:13,14 *Amp.***

Notice that the prescribed instrument for discipline in all these verses is "the rod." The Bible doesn't say the belt would drive foolishness far from the heart of a child, and it never mentions a leather strap, either.

I've seen parents use their hand to discipline their children. If you've ever seen children flinch when you reach out to pat them on the head, you know they've been slapped or hit. Parents, our hands are supposed to be used to love and embrace.

Immediate Behavior vs. Eternal Heart Change

Why do parents use flyswatters, rulers, electric cords,

tools, wooden spoons, shoes, and so forth? Usually parents get so frustrated with their child's foolishness or repeated disrespect, they grab anything close and start swinging.

My mother once chased my brother all over the neighborhood with a five-pound, black cast iron skillet! She never caught him! It was hilarious. My sister and I laughed so hard, we cried. Finally, my mother dropped the pan and fell on the ground laughing at herself and what the neighbors must be thinking.

My family took our annual trek back to Oklahoma during the summer. There were four children, Mom, Dad, and our 125-pound Saint Bernard. Dad would remove the back seat, and we'd all pile into our four-door Pontiac. We'd have to roll the windows down or run the defogger, because Dad couldn't see to drive otherwise. It was a circus!

My brother and I would have championship wrestling in the enlarged back seat. Of course, we'd get too rowdy, and Dad would tell us over and over again to settle down. That went on and on until Dad would run out of patience.

He wore a college class ring that he'd spin on his finger and ping us on the head with. Those were my first experiences of being "slain in the spirit." It would knock your equilibrium out of kilter! I wouldn't be normal again for 30 minutes.

When Dad disciplined us with that class ring, it altered our behavior. In fact, it affected *more* than our behavior! (We could have been called knot-heads, and it would have been an accurate description.)

My Dad stopped our disobedient behavior, but it didn't affect our hearts (just our heads). Too often parents are looking for the immediate gratification of behavior change, not at the eternal picture.

We read that the rod of correction drives foolishness out of the heart of a child. The Hebrew word for "foolishness" can be translated as "rebellion." Only the rod can drive rebellion out of a heart! Not only is rebellion driven out, but wisdom is imparted (Proverbs 29:15, *NIV*).

Divine Disciplinary Dealings

It is good for a man that he bear the yoke [of divine disciplinary dealings] in his youth.

Lamentations 3:27 *Amp.*

It is a *divine* thing when the rebellion that exists in a child is driven out by the simple act of discipline. However, there is a vast difference between divine disciplinary dealings and what most Christian parents are administering.

I want you to get a new image in your mind — a Biblical picture — of what transpires when you correct your child God's way. As you discipline with the rod of correction, the Lord drives out foolishness and replaces it with His wisdom (Proverbs 22:15; 29:15).

If you are a Christian, I'm sure you've been baptized in water. My question is: Does the water you're baptized in save you? No! Does the water possess the miraculous action that transforms you from spiritual death to spiritual life? No! It's not the water, it's *the act of obedience* to God's Word. It's the same with divine discipline: The power is not in the rod, but in your obedience to God's Word.

I've seen parents get so angry, they tried to drive the foolishness out of their child by swinging the rod so hard, they'd drive the child's head through sheet rock. It's not in the strength of the parent's *stroke*, but in the strength of the parent's *heart*.

Only God Can Extract the Rebellion

God is the One who extracts the rebellion. God is the One who imparts His wisdom. And God is love (1 John 4:8). Love engages God in the correction process. God gets involved in discipline when you are motivated by love, not by anger, embarrassment, or frustration. When you mix God's Word with God's love, you can't lose! It is divine.

The tool, the rod, is important, but it's more important how you use the rod and in what spirit you use it to impact the behavior of your children.

I won't argue that slapping your children for wrong doing will alter their behavior for the moment, but it won't change their *heart* eternally. Divine disciplinary dealings reach to the innermost parts of the heart.

> **Blows that wound cleanse away evil, and strokes [for correction] reach to the innermost parts.**
>
> **Proverbs 20:30 *Amp.***

So it's when the Lord reaches the heart of your child that permanent change occurs. When we are in control of ourself and we are truly motivated by God's love as we correct our children, God cleanses away the evil of rebellion from their inward parts. The Lord is so good! We saw that He not only removes the stubbornness, but He imparts His wisdom.

> **Length of days is in her [wisdom's] right hand; and in her left hand riches and honor.**
>
> **Her ways are ways of pleasantness, and all her paths are peace.**
>
> **Proverbs 3:16,17**

As we carefully discipline our "little blessings" with the rod of correction, we are giving God the opportunity to place the outward benefits of wisdom into their lives. Pleasantness and peace would be worth the entire struggle of child-rearing, but the Lord doesn't stop here; He also adds to children whose parents have trained them to obey through the rod, length of days (long life) as well as riches and honor! There is so much more happening when we respond to our children's disobedience *carefully*.

There is an art to skillful discipline . It is an art that must be learned and developed. We teach child-training seminars all across the country, and we jokingly say to the parents that we should change the name to "Parent-Training Seminar," because the *real* discipline comes as Christian parents marshall their own emotions to do what's best for their offspring.

Shaping Future Generations

Raising children is an awesome task. It isn't easy, because you never get off work. Often you become taxed from the daily grind and wonder if it is worth the effort. Yes, it is! You are shaping future generations.

God has entrusted these awesome talents into your hands to shape and mold through His love and wisdom. If He has entrusted them to you, He must believe in you. He must trust you. He has given His Spirit to help you (John 14:16).

Lean on the Lord when you become weary. Seek His strength. Talk to your mate about your children. As you communicate your desires, dreams, and goals with one another and come into agreement together, you'll find that the encouragement you receive from each other will motivate you toward excellence.

Roxanne and I talk regularly about how *we* can improve one area or another in our parenting. We always come to an agreement whether or not we should discipline our children for a specific act or attitude. We do nothing until we can see clearly what should be done.

If you're a single parent, you'll really have to develop dependency on the Holy Spirit. But that's good, not bad! Cultivate a friendship with someone with whom you can communicate concerning your children.

This person should not be someone who will put you down for expecting obedience all the time, but someone who will fellowship with you along Biblical lines; someone who will inspire you to stay consistent in "AAA treatment" and in discipline.

Some people are disciplinarians by nature. Their standards are often too high. Their expectations are unreasonable for the age of the child. On the other hand, there are people who are too lenient of whatever their children's behavior might be. They have no standards for their children. Locate and nurture the friendship of those whose goals are similar to yours.

Seven Guidelines in Discipline

Guideline 1: Always be in contol. We expect our children to control their emotions when they've been wronged by a friend or relative, yet we fly off the handle and say and do things to our "little blessings" that we later regret. Why? Because we're not in control.

I've observed mothers swoop down on their children like an eagle toward its prey. They grab the child by one arm and, in mid-air, swat him on the behind. The child doesn't know what hit him unless his mom acts this way regularly.

Don't allow your children's misbehavior to rattle you. Anger, frustration, or embarrassment are not the motives that engage God in your discipline. Never discipline with the attitude, "You embarrassed me in the grocery store, so take that!" Or, "I can't believe you did that at your grandmother's house!"

It's not our children we're thinking about in these situations; it's our pride — what others will think about us in the light of what Johnny has done. It's called selfishness. If your motive is to have well-behaved children so all will know you're a superior species called "Super Mom," your actions are built on a crumbling foundation.

On the other hand, if you only resort to "the rod" as a last-ditch effort to straighten out your son, you'll still be losing. Remember, it's obedience to the Word — not just the rod. God wants you to have your emotions and actions in absolute control. . . cool and calm!

The rod in the hand of an angry or frustrated parent is no different than any other instrument of cruelty. You will beat your children if your discipline is done in anger.

Using the right instrument (rod) with the wrong attitude doesn't make it right; it's still child abuse!

I found myself increasingly frustrated as one of our children disobeyed in the same area time and time again. Then the Lord spoke to my heart and said, "Rejoice every time your child receives correction. Each correction enables you to drive foolishness and rebellion out of their life." Whatever is left when they become adults will contend with them until they bring it into submission.

I don't know about you, but as an adult, it is a tedious process to gain victory over the desires of the flesh. I want to help my children overcome as much as possible so they can reach adulthood running and not stumbling.

Children have an easier time learning foreign languages than adults do. If they're subjected to another culture, they'll learn that language unconsciously. They learn so they can communicate with their playmates. It's the same with God's Word in their life. My children don't even know we're training them in God's ways, because they know no other way!

Every time you drive foolishness far from your children, think of yourself as hitting home runs for Jesus! When their peers are struggling with various decisions, your children will effortlessly make the right choices.

Guideline 2: Always deal with disobedience as quickly as possible! The younger children are, the sooner you need to address disobedience when it occurs. If you don't deal with their misbehavior immediately, they won't be able to relate to the correction.

Guideline 3: The parent who sees or hears the disobedience is the one who should deal with it!

Dad arrives home from a long day at the office, grabs the dip and chips, and heads for the recliner. He then flips through the TV channels, holding the remote control in one hand and a tall soft drink in the other.

Suddenly World War III breaks out next to him! He screams at his wife to settle the fight between the children, who are interrupting his entertainment. He says, "Honey, I've worked twelve hours today with no peace, and I'd like to relax, please."

His wife is bouncing the infant on her hip as she finishes dinner. I'd like to ask him this question: "Hey, Champ, what has your wife been doing for the last twelve hours herself?"

I've stayed home with the children for the day, and I was *elated* to go back to work. I thank God that He gave Roxanne the grace to stay home with our three "little blessings." Yet when I arrive home, it's *our* job to train them in the way they should go. I delegate the responsibility to her while I am absent from home, but once I'm present, it's a team effort.

I don't put my wife down by speaking disparagingly about our children. If there is an attitude problem in one of the children, it's not Roxanne's fault or responsibility to change it; it's our job together, for we're a team! We win together, work together, and rejoice together.

When Dad comes home from a long, difficult day, he would *like* to be greeted at the door by all his cheering fans (his wife and children). He wants to see his beauty queen (wife) dressed fit to kill, and the subjects of his kingdom (children) awaiting him with hugs, kisses, and all the benefits a king deserves.

Too often, however, no one is awaiting him with outstretched arms. He enters the house only to find his wife with her hair half combed. She's dragging from exhaustion and looks as if she could faint at any moment.

She sighs with relief as she says, "Thank God you're finally home! The children have been driving me up the wall. I told them, 'When your father gets home, he'll deal with you!'" No wonder it's so quiet in the house. The children vacated the premises in hopes of delaying the inevitable.

Daddy is viewed as the bad guy. When they hear his car pull into the driveway, they split! They've either gone out the back door to their friend's house or off to their favorite hiding place.

Mothers, you must regain your children's respect (honor). The parent who sees or hears the misbehavior has the glorious opportunity to impart wisdom once more!

Guideline 4: We correct a wrong choice, but we are not to tear down a child's self-image. In discipline we must convey the thought, "You're a good boy who chose to do the wrong thing."

Never say, "What's wrong with you? Do you have brain damage? If I've told you once, I've told you a thousand times... You're so stupid. You're just like your mother's family — dumb! You can't be my son. No son of mine would do such an ignorant thing! You'll never amount to anything. Your sister never does this. Why can't you be like her?"

When we correct our children's mistakes, they should leave our time of discipline with a belief that they can make the right decision next time.

I want my children to believe in their God-given ability to choose the right path. Our life is composed of choices. The whole sum of where we are, whom we did or didn't marry, is based on choices. You chose Jesus as your Lord and Savior. You decided to read this book. Everything you will accomplish in this lifetime began with a choice.

Train your children that their choices will either bring them happiness, peace, and fulfillment or heartache, misery, and disappointment.

Always project a sense of worth to your children through your attitudes, words, and actions. Tell them you believe in them. Endear them to you! One of the meanings of "son" in the Hebrew is "builder of the family name. To make or repair." Tell your children you are proud to be their father or mother. One day they'll display their pride in being your offspring.

Guideline 5: There is a difference between punishment and discipline. *Punishment* is payback. Punishment is satisfied when the recipient suffers for how he's made you suffer. *Discipline* is something you do *for* your children, not *to* them. Discipline is satisfied when the recipient changes course from sin into obedience.

The goal of our discipline is for our children to accurately govern themselves. Our intent is not to make them dependent on us, but confident enough of their choices to follow decision with determination. Our aim is that our children will become self-disciplined to the extent that when they're out of our presence they'll do what they believe, not just what their mother or father believes.

Guideline 6: Discipline is more important than fellowship with others. What's the higher priority: conversation with a friend, or the training of your offspring? I've observed men talking about the football game after church while their "little blessings" are sorely disobeying! Dad snaps his fingers once, then twice, not at the child, but at his wife, in an attempt to get her attention to deal with their brat...I mean, blessing.

Mom may be on the telephone talking with Miss Spiritual from the church, discussing how wonderful their lessons have been in the Adult Sunday School Class while Johnny is in gross disobedience.

Mom wouldn't dare hang up the phone to correct Johnny. Why, that would be an unpardonable sin. So she gives her son hand signals to try to stop him. She may even go so far as to throw something at him, but she never considers cutting off the conversation with her friend and dealing with Johnny.

Guideline 7: The greatest allies in discipline are consistency and repetition. Rather than acknowledging the child's sin, you act as if it didn't happen. You spare the rod. Remember, "He that spareth his rod hateth his son...."

It would be better not to use the rod of correction at all than to be inconsistent. Once you're convinced that the rod is the way to correct disobedience, get ready to be tempted with inconsistency.

We have our children for eighteen years. If you will approach the child-rearing process with a correct evaluation of time, it will keep you from trying to get overnight results or giving up during the second week. We're to bring them up — which is a process, a maturing, a growth.

If you'll start when they're young, time, repetition, and consistency are on your side. This form of discipline doesn't fail; it's parents who don't consistently apply God's Word who experience failure.

In life, responsibility falls on the shoulders of people. You can have the greatest organizational structure with lazy people, and the greatest organization will fail. Yet you may have a clumsy, unorganized structure with motivated people, and the organization will thrive.

When you put the best way together with motivated, concerned parents, you have a winning combination.

Children learn at a higher rate than we give them credit for. Just because your children may not be able to articulate what they're learning doesn't mean they don't understand you.

Roxanne and I repeatedly affirmed to Janae that the reason we disciplined her when she disobeyed was because we loved her: "he who loves...[his son] is careful to discipline him" (Proverbs 13:24 *NIV*).

Once while we were fellowshipping with other families, the children were being disobedient. Janae was two years old at the time. She came and stood close to me and said, "Daddy, don't their mommy and daddy love them?" It hit me like a ton of bricks.

Janae had observed these children being disobedient to their parents, yet their parents were not disciplining them. The parents continued to tell them to stop and threatened them again and again.

What I saw was twentieth century parents being normal. Janae saw parents who didn't love their children. Repetition was working for us. Yet I'd never before heard Janae say that she understood what I'd said or done. That night I was convinced that children learn quicker than they can communicate.

Seven Things That Provoke Children to Wrath

Ephesians 6:4 states, "And, ye fathers, provoke not your children to wrath...."

There are seven areas in discipline that can provoke wrath and anger in a child instead of the desire to please.

1. Inconsistency to discipline.

Effective discipline cannot be built on mood swings. One day you're in a good mood, so your children's misbehavior is overlooked. Tomorrow you're not as chipper, so you come down on them for accidents rather than disobedience.

Only discipline your children for direct rebellion to your words, not for accidentally spilling their glass of milk at the table. Love, not moodiness, is the premise and basis for successful training. Children cannot maintain consistency in obedience if parents are not consistent.

Children receive conflicting signals when parents become strict around various adults whom Mom or Dad want to impress. Never discipline verbally or corporally for the sake of another adult. If your motive isn't for your child's betterment, he or she will see right through your hypocrisy and will ultimately be provoked to wrath!

So don't change around "special people." Be consistent for the truly special people in your life — your children. Our goal is to make lasting impressions on our children, not on our friends.

Favoritism among siblings *often* results in bad relationships among brothers and sisters. It also clouds their attitude toward God's character and His feelings toward them. Our heavenly Father is no respecter of persons. As God's representatives, we should try with all our strength to imitate His example.

If you discipline the oldest for wrongdoing, you should discipline the youngest for wrongdoing. Through training children to obey your voice rather than the 112 commandments of your house, even the smallest child can be responsible for his choices. Of course, what you'll require the oldest daughter to do will differ from what you require from her younger sister, but the fundamentals apply to all age groups.

Favoritism is not a healthy practice. You'll have to work hard on this aspect of child-rearing in order to be fair. For example, Roxanne and I noticed that for a time we had allowed our second child, Jason, to get away with disobedience that Janae, our first, never dreamed of doing.

It is human nature. But in neglecting to discipline him, we were hurting Jason, for we were allowing him to be inconsistent in obedience. This, in time, will alter his pursuit of the plan of God for his life. And we don't want him to be inconsistent to obey God!

Our reasoning for overlooking his disobedience was, "He is so cute and adorable." He'd say something that would make us all laugh. He'd look at us with those big blue eyes and we'd melt. Regardless, we were doing him an injustice by ignoring his disobedience.

The promise of Ephesians 6:3 pivots off the condition in Ephesians 6:1,2. If we're consistent in lovingly requiring our child's honor and obedience to our authority, God is able to consistently ensure that child's well-being and long life!

2. Disciplining for things you do yourself.

The old saying, "Do what I say, not what I do" won't endure the eighteen years of child training. Young children will do what you say, but as they get older, they'll do what you *do*.

The problem is compounded when you discipline your son for something you do. If you preach, "Don't drink alcohol," you shouldn't drink it. If you don't want your children to watch R-rated movies, you shouldn't watch them. If you want your children to respect their mother and father, you'd better respect yours. If you want your children to value your mate's opinions, then you must. Sons usually reflect their father's attitude toward their mother.

Wrath is provoked in children, not because you expect

more from them than other parents expect, but for expecting higher standards than you yourself practice!

In Genesis 18:19, the Lord said that Abraham would command his children "after him." Abraham commanded his children to follow his example of obedience. The Apostle Paul told the Church at Thessalonica, "Follow me as I follow Christ." Can you say to your children, "Follow what I do"? Can you boldly say, "Follow me as I follow Christ"?

At times, the change begins with us before it filters down to our offspring! I'm not preaching parental perfection, although I am saying you should not discipline children with the rod of correction for sins you yourself commit.

If you blow it in front of them, be man or woman enough to admit it and seek their forgiveness. It ministers to them to see you humble yourself and repent when you sin. What blesses them is not that you sinned, but that you repented and did all in your power to rectify it.

3. Disciplining in front of others.

I've observed women berating their husbands in front of their friends, and the husbands becoming furious with them. No one likes to be put down in front of others. Children are people, too! They have the same emotional needs as adults.

Never discipline your children at the expense of their self-esteem. Humiliation provokes immediate wrath. Divine disciplinary dealings won't strip a person's dignity. The old saying, "Praise in public, correct in private" is so true! Also keep the Golden Rule in mind: "Do unto others as you would have them do unto you." Don't discipline verbally or with the rod in the presence of relatives, friends, or any others.

Once while walking through a shopping mall, we saw a mother forehand her 6-year-old son on the back of the head. The child grabbed his head as he looked at everyone staring at him. The paramount issue wasn't the physical pain from his injury, but the pain in his heart from being disgraced publicly.

4. Disciplining for things they didn't know were wrong.

If your daughter says she didn't know that it was wrong to do such and such, believe her. You'll have all the opportunities you'll ever want to use the rod. If you persist in disciplining her at this point, and she vehemently argues that she's telling the truth, you'll provoke her to wrath. Instead, tell her, "You must understand from now on that it's wrong to do the thing you said you didn't know was wrong."

The most productive discipline is when your children cooperate. Discipline reaches their hearts when they know they've chosen to disobey and yield to the correction. (Don't misunderstand — no one looks forward to being disciplined, but there is a difference between accepting and fighting against the correction.)

It's not the best time to discipline when your "little blessing" is slinging his arms and screaming in anger. First, your discipline won't reach his heart and, second, it will only add to his frustration. Trying to discipline while your son is displaying anger will only get you angry!

If the incident happens in a public setting, get him out of there as quickly as possible. I'm not saying you should allow him to disrupt the gathering or destroy a store display; I am saying you won't make any progress disciplining him when he's emotionally out of control. Get him settled down first. Then you can properly communicate.

5. Disciplining in anger.

Inevitably, you will discipline your offspring harshly if you are angry. If you proceed in anger, you're likely to hit them in the wrong place.

The buttocks is the largest muscle on your entire body. A child can absorb the strokes from the rod, if disciplined on the bottom. Strokes for correction should be administered on their buttocks, not on their legs or back. When angry, most parents just swing, hoping to connect somewhere.

Discipline your son while there is hope, but do not [indulge your angry resentments by undue chastisements and] set yourself to his ruin.

Proverbs 19:18 *Amp.*

When parents discipline in anger, they throw the process in reverse and begin losing ground instead of making progress in obedience. *When you discipline your child in anger, he sees your error, not his own.* When you enforce your rules in anger, your child focuses on your sin instead of his. I want my child to face his choice — his decision to rebel — but that inspection of himself is impossible when my sin (anger) is screaming louder than his own conscience.

He who loves his son is careful to discipline him. You must be careful in what spirit you're disciplining your son. You will hit too hard if you're angry. Remember, it's love, not anger, that reaches the inward parts of the heart. It's not the strength of the stroke, but the strength of the heart that insures eternal change.

I quote Proverbs 13:24 every time I discipline our children. Jason knows that Daddy's strokes are harder than Mom's, so he often says, "Daddy, be careful." What he means is, "Don't hit me too hard."

6. Discussing their disobedience with others.

I, even I, am he that blotteth out thy transgressions for mine own sake, and will not remember thy sins.

Isaiah 43:25

When we repent to God, confessing our sins, He is faithful and just to forgive us and cleanse us from all our unrighteousness (1 John 1:9). We are so blessed that God not only forgives our sins, but He doesn't even remember them!

When our children are disciplined with the rod, they pray and repent to the Lord afterwards. Roxanne and I assure them that we forgive them, too. Then we don't bring up the subject of their misbehavior again.

You will send your children mixed signals if you jokingly tell others about their disobedience. They won't believe you when you tell them you've forgiven them, and they'll doubt that God really forgives them as well. The older they become, the more hurtful such experiences are.

If they are good children, they won't want others to know about their mistakes. I'm sure you don't want people telling everyone the blunders of *your* past. Why? You don't want others to view you in light of one or two failures. Neither do your children! The only other person who has a right to know about their disobedience is your mate. When you share with one another it should always be done in private and kept in strict confidence.

7. Never recognizing what the child does right.

You are destined to provoke your children to wrath if you only see their mistakes and not their achievements.

For example, if you scream, "I caught you! I caught you," your son or daughter will quickly scan their previous actions — just like you do when seeing a policeman. You immediately check your speedometer and your seat belt.

Instead, scream, "I caught you! I caught you!" As paranoia covers your child's face, say, "I caught you doing something *good*!" Shout! Scream! Hit the wall! Dance around! Get more excited over what your children do right than what they do wrong. It's easy to get angry. You don't have to work at being upset. It's like growing weeds: You never have to plant or water them; they just grow! But you do have to make yourself act crazy over good behavior. Don't say, "It's not normal for me to get emotional." Obviously! That's the very reason it turns your kids on! They know you're working at it! You're trying!

But if you only acknowledge sin, not victory, your children will give up trying to please you. Their attitude will be, "Obey my parents — so what?" Is it too much to ask that you'd *try* to improve your reward system?

I expect my children to work at obedience every day of their life. I'm convinced that the true problem is that most parents aren't attuned to their children's obedience — only their disobedience. Our parental "radar system" never picks up the good, only the "enemy aircraft" called "rebellion."

If you would ask God to open your eyes to see the good, you would have many opportunities every day to express your approval. And when your children receive a sufficient measure of praise, they will want more and more praise, until obedience becomes a pleasure, not a struggle, for them. But when children don't care anymore what their parents think, wrath has taken the rightful place of honor.

The Art of Discipline

The art of discipline is a skill that is learned. It is similar to any skill: It is developed by consistent application of proven techniques.

The Psalmist in Psalm 127:4 refers to raising children as a mighty warrior who uses his bow and arrow in battle. To hit the bull's eye in archery takes practice, patience, and a desire to master the art. To master the art of discipline, one must be careful — skillful — *when* he disciplines, in what *attitude, where, around whom, with what* instrument, and *how* as well as *why.*

With the information you've received in previous pages, coupled with the assistance of the Holy Spirit and your God-given common sense, you are ready to walk through the steps of actually applying the rod of correction.

Addressing Willfull Disobedience

When your "little blessing" willfully disobeys your voice, what should your first move be: Strangle him until he turns every shade of red? Of course not. Very politely take him to a private place where it's unlikely you'll be interrupted.

Treat this as a personal, intimate time. This major event should be approached carefully. Try not to send off signals to everyone else that "Mama's on the war path and little

Johnny's scalp will be removed." Often people wonder why Roxanne left the room and where she went. The truth is, she left to discipline one of our children privately.

Your child's dignity should be intact before, during, and after his discipline. The bathroom is usually a private place. In public places, it's not proper unless you're able to lock the door and be alone. Be discreet for your child's sake as well as your own. Other people don't know you're disciplining in love. They see that rod, and their first thought is child abuse!

Roxanne, Janae and I were riding an elevator in a hotel in El Paso, Texas. Roxanne was carrying the rod of correction under her arm with her purse. When an older woman boarded the elevator, her eyes got big and she asked, pointing to the rod, "That thing is not for her?" Roxanne smiled and said, "It's sure not for me!" (She now carries a purse-sized rod.)

Choosing To Do What's Right

After arriving at the private place, get eye level with your child and say, "I am not happy with your choice." Let him or her see in your eyes your displeasure with their decision.

Usually it's not wise to ask them why they did it. It only opens the door to shift the blame or to lie. Usually the root cause of their misbehavior is foolishness or rebellion. At times it's appropriate to ask for an explanation, but most often it is a dead end. (See point five under Guidelines for Discipline.)

After your child has seen your displeasure with his choice, then explain why he should choose to do what is right. (Your lightning-fast mind immediately asks, "Why should he do what's right?") There are two broad reasons, scripturally and personally.

Scripturally, it's to please God. Your child's obedience to parental authority is a direct commandment of God. Your child's willing compliance not only pleases God, but

God also rewards his obedience with long life and continued well-being.

Television commercials attempt to sell us on the benefits of the product being promoted. Businesses spend millions of dollars for elaborate production and air time to lure consumers to buy, and it works.

We need to use their methods of selling (communicating the benefits) to promote our product (obedience). Be creative! What are some things your children want to become, do, have, see, experience? If these dreams are wholesome, tell them that God wants to help them achieve their desires. By honoring and obeying you, they are enabling God to fulfill His promises to them. Explain to them that obedience opens the door to our heavenly Father and closes the door to the devil!

Personally, tell your children how it makes you feel when they choose to obey you the first time they are spoken to. Share how it blesses you. Too often the real image parents are conveying is, "Just get out of my hair! Leave me alone. Go do your own thing. Just don't get pregnant, and don't break the law." If you sincerely mean that it blesses you when your children obey you, your honesty and repetition will create the desire to please you.

Assure the Child of Your Love

Next, assure your children of your love. Tell them that the reason you discipline them when they rebel is because you love them (Proverbs 13:24). I tell my daughter, "I'm not using the rod on you because I'm mad, but the Bible says if I love you I'll be careful to, and I genuinely love you! Do you believe that I love you?" She responds positively.

Receiving the Strokes

I then position the child to receive the strokes. With smaller children, you might place them where they can either hold onto something secure, like a chair, slightly bent over, with their buttocks raised to give you a clear target. Older ones can hold onto a counter top or table. Don't make them lay across a bed to receive discipline.

Three strokes are sufficient. We don't suggest that you give more strokes for "worse" disobedience. There's no such thing as "not-so-bad" sin and "really bad" sin. Sin is sin in the sight of God. Mom, if your sons snicker after being disciplined, then strengthen, don't lengthen the strokes. Three is my suggestion.

Maintaining the Child's Dignity

Parents ask if they should discipline their children's bare bottom. I respond with two questions: Is there dignity in dropping your drawers? Mom, when your son is 15 years old, will you require him to remove his pants? The answer is no! I've had mothers quickly retort, "But it gets their attention when I discipline this way!"

I'm sure it does. We definitely want our discipline to be such that when our offspring is presented with a choice to disobey, their bottom will speak loud and clear, "It is better to obey." Yet I believe that bare-bottom discipline puts more emphasis on the pain inflicted than on our faith in God's operation. To me it borders on child abuse. Our goal is to help, not hurt.

After you've used the rod of correction, immediately embrace the child. Never send him away, saying, "Go to your room and think about it. Get out of my sight!" God's welcome sign stays lit. His arms are open to us even when we've sinned. Embracing your child is non-verbal communication. It says, loud and clear, "Even though you missed the mark, I love you and believe in you."

Lead the Child in Repentance

While holding or embracing the child, have him repent to God for breaking His commandment. If your child is too small to pray on his own, you lead him in prayer.

First John 1:9 is our favorite scripture in repentance. We might pray something like, "Father, in Jesus' Name I confess

I (name the disobedience). I repent for disobeying You. First John 1:9 says that if I'd confess my sins, You'd be faithful and just to forgive me and cleanse me from all unrighteousness. Thank You for forgiving me. In Jesus' Name, Amen!"

We've repeated that so often, it wasn't long before the children needed no more help in reciting it.

Make Discipline a Positive Experience

When we open our eyes after the last "amen," I look my child in the eye and say, "I forgive you." There are times we leave the place of discipline more endeared to one another than before the misbehavior.

Don't allow your children to leave this time of discipline believing they're terrible, no-good children. They can and should leave with the belief that next time they'll do what is right. They'll believe in their ability to obey and please you because you believe in them.

Good Judgment Is Necessary

Throughout this chapter, you've read guidelines and principles designed to govern your approach to discipline. Yet with all these rules, judgment to apply them is the necessary ingredient that brings success.

For many years, I refereed basketball. Throughout the years, I've observed other officials who were students of the rules, yet they lacked judgment when put into the game situations. The fans, coaches, and players stayed frustrated. I'm sure if you enjoy watching sporting events, you've gotten upset with officials a time or two yourself!

Some referees make mistakes for a lack of knowledge of the rules, while others miss it in the ability to interpret the rules as the game unfolds.

Let's pray together that as the game of life unfolds for our children, we'll exercise godly judgment to know when to blow our whistle and call a foul and when to let them continue to play the game.

Chapter 4
Home Is the Key

Proverbs 22:6 says, "Train up a child in the way he should go; and when he is old, he will not depart from it."

I grew up in a church where this verse was quoted quite often. The parents' version of this verse always was that if you train children up right, they may go out into the world, but they will eventually come back to the Lord.

But the scripture says to train up a child in the way he should go, and when he is old, he will not depart from it. This means your child will *never* leave it!

Our Guarantee From God

We have a guarantee from God that we can raise our children according to HIS standard, according to HIS way, and we will never have to watch them "go out and come back." We will never have to watch them go out into the world and wonder if they will come back to the house of God — *because they will never depart from their faith in God in the first place!*

The word "train" means "to create a desire, or to oversee that what you've taught is being done." So let's read it that way: "Create a desire in your child in the way he should go, and when he is old, he will not depart from it."

This is what the Word of God teaches concerning rearing your children. If I were to train you, I would tell you what the Word says, and then I'd go home with you and see that you did it.

Many of us have taught our children well in most areas,

79

but we haven't taken the time to train them that once we have issued a command — once we have given instructions to them — we will follow through to make sure they're doing what we told them to do. We're to see that they do the things we've told them to do.

We're to create a desire within them to please. In the margin of *Dake's Annotated Reference Bible*, Finis Jennings Dake says, "Train up or hedge in a child in the way he should go, and when his responsibility to stay in it comes, he will do so. The idea seems to be that when the child comes to this opening of the way, he will have had a complete series of instructions on every step he is to take. You are to drill him thoroughly on how to perform his duties, how to escape danger, and how to appropriate the blessings of the way. Stamp these lessons deep on his soul and lead him to practice them until they are a part of his life and nature. Bathe him in prayer and instill the fear of God into him (which is to love righteousness and hate iniquity), and he shall not depart from it. *It is an unfailing law.*"

As parents, we must make a decision that we are going to drill the Word of God into our children to a point that they don't know anything else.

I know that many of you who have taken steps to train your children in the way God wants you to, have been accused of brainwashing your children. People have accused me of this. They've said, "I understand what you're saying, but it just seems to me like you're *brainwashing* your child."

Brainwashing or Renewing?

If that's the word they want to use, that's fine with me, because God said we're to renew our minds, and that's all we're doing with our children: We're taking the garbage that the world would like to put in their minds, and in its place we're putting the Word of God, so their very life and nature will be to walk according to the will and Word of God.

It's up to us to instill the Word of God in our children. We must stamp these lessons deep on their soul and *lead* them to practice them. We're to *lead* our children into practicing the Word to where it becomes a part of their life and nature.

More instructions about child-rearing are found in Proverbs 31. These verses are from *The Amplified Bible:*

"The words of Lemuel, king of Massa, which his mother taught him" (v. 1). So these were the words of a mother. She says, "A capable, intelligent and virtuous woman, who is he who can find her?" Let's change the word "woman" to "mother" for this study:

"A capable, intelligent and virtuous *mother,* who is he who can find her? She is far more precious than jewels, and her value is far above rubies or pearls...

"She girds herself with strength [spiritual, mental and physical fitness for her God-given task] and makes her arms strong and firm...

"Strength and dignity are her clothing and her position is strong and secure. She rejoices over the future — the latter day or time to come [knowing that she and her family are in readiness for it]!

"She opens her mouth with skillful and godly Wisdom, and on her tongue is the law of kindness — giving counsel and instruction.

"She looks well to how things go in her household, and the bread of idleness...she will not eat.

"Her children rise up and call her blessed...and her husband boasts of and praises her...." (vv. 10,17,25-28).

The "God-Given Task"

We saw in verse 17 that "She girds herself with strength... for her God-given task." It is *a God-given task* to be a mother! Too often in modern society, when women are asked, "What do you do for a living?" they reply, "I'm *just* a mother," or, "I'm *just* a housewife."

But "mother" is a *God-given* task. I admire those mothers who work outside the home. I read an article that said the average mother works a minimum of 80 hours a week.

Imagine the hours a *working* mother puts in!

God wants to help us in our God-given task of being a mother. He wants us to gird ourself with strength from Him, because that's the only way we can be that "virtuous mother" He's speaking of here in the thirty-first chapter of Proverbs.

God says the virtuous mother girds herself with strength from Him — not strength that she gets from herself, or strength that she musters from soap operas and doing things around the house — but strength that she gets from God.

And it's this strength that we're to give to our children. But if we don't take time to first *get* that strength from God, we won't have anything to give our children! We'll have days when we're frustrated and worn out by noon! But if we'll take time apart every day to give ourself to God, He will give of Himself to us. And that's what we give to our children.

Verse 25 says, "Strength and dignity are her clothing and her position is strong and secure. She rejoices over the future...knowing that she and her family are in readiness for it."

Preparing for the Future

The only way you can know you're ready for the future is when you've gotten yourself ready. The only way you can know that your children are ready for the future is when *you've* prepared them for it. *You've* given them the strength that you received from God, and *you've* made them to be ready to face whatever comes their way.

Verse 26 says of the virtuous mother, "She opens her mouth with skillful and godly Wisdom...." We're not quiet, meek, humble little women who don't say or know anything. We're strong. Our position is secure. We open our mouth with skillful and godly wisdom.

Again, we can't open our mouth with skillful and godly wisdom if we haven't first put the Word in our heart. If we haven't taken time to put it *within* us, then it can't come *out* of us.

Verse 26 in its entirety reads, "She opens her mouth with skillful and godly Wisdom, and on her tongue is the law of kindness — giving counsel and instruction."

"The Law of Kindness"

We must speak *kind* words to our children. We must learn that when we give our children instructions and counsel, it should be in a setting of kindness.

It's never fun or easy to obey someone who *yells* at you. In fact, the first thing you want to do is exactly *opposite* of what they tell you to do, whether it's your friend, your neighbor, your boss, or parent.

But when words of kindness are spoken, it creates a desire within you to *please* and *obey* that person, doing anything he or she asks you to do.

So "the law of kindness" should be on our tongue; in every word we speak to our children.

Little Hearts Are Tender

Also, be careful how you speak their name. Children's little hearts are so tender, and they need to hear words of kindness. They hear enough "junk words" wherever else they go. They need to hear Mom and Dad speak words of kindness, words that embrace them.

Give your children counsel and instruction with words of kindness, not with words of frustration, words that imply, "I wish you weren't here," words that imply, "I'm tired of you," or words that show, "I've had a bad day."

Don't take out on your children what you've missed in life, or what you've messed up today.

In Second Timothy 1:5, Paul was writing to his spiritual son, Timothy, telling him that he longed to see him. We read in *The Amplified Bible:*

"I am calling up memories of your sincere and unqualified faith [the leaning of your entire personality on God in Christ in absolute trust and confidence in His power, wisdom and goodness, a faith] that first lived permanently in (the heart of) your grandmother Lois and you mother Eunice and now, I am [fully] persuaded, (dwells) in you also."

Righteousness Through Generations

What was this? It was the *righteousness* that was coming down through the generations. And even though we know from the writings in the Bible that Paul was Timothy's spiritual father, Paul didn't boast of it himself.

Instead, he told Timothy, "The thing that has caused you to stand — the quality that has put you over in life — is the faith you learned from your mother and your grandmother."

We have a great responsibility to our children. It shouldn't be left up to our pastor, Sunday school teacher, or children's church worker to instill faith into our children. That's our responsibility, but with this responsibility comes rewards.

What a thrill we will receive when our children are adults and come home and say, "Mama, the reason I'm making it is because of you; because of the things you put into me as a child."

That's what Paul recognized in Timothy. He could look at Timothy's grandmother and mother and say, "You're just like them, Timothy. The stability they put into you is what put you over in life." Paul also mentioned "...the leaning of your entire personality on God." Is the leaning of your entire personality on God, His power, and His goodness the same as brainwashing?

Hold Your Children Close

In Psalm 22:9, David is speaking to God. He said, "You made me trust in You even at my mother's breasts." I believe with all my heart that God ordained breastfeeding for many different reasons. When you breastfeed, a special closeness develops between you and your baby. This special time is over all too soon. When these days are gone, what happens next?

If we will continue to *hold* our children close to us, to *love* them, and show *affection* for them, it will help them trust in God. David said it caused him to trust in God. The trust and the confidence he gained from the closeness he felt to his mother caused him to trust in God!

We can see from this that our responsibilities for loving and giving ourselves to our children as a mother are great. Our actions may determine the degree our child learns to love and trust God!

God's Promises Will Never Fail

My son, keep your father's [God-given] commandment, and forsake not the law of [God] your mother [taught you].

Bind them continually upon your heart, and tie them about your neck.

When you go, [the Word of your parents' God] it shall lead you; when you sleep, it shall keep you, and when you waken, it shall talk with you.

For the commandment is a lamp, and the whole teaching of the law is light, and reproofs of discipline are the way of life.

Proverbs 6:20-23 *Amp.*

The Bible says that heaven and earth will pass away, but the Word of God will stand forever (Matthew 5:18). The Word will always be... Even when we can't be there for our children, God can.

After our daughter, Janae, had been in kindergarten for two weeks, she looked at me one morning as I was helping her make her bed, and she said, "Mama, I really hate to ask you this, but I'm just going to have to do it."

I replied, "Well, what is it, honey?"

And she said, "*Please* don't ever call me 'baby' in front of my school friends anymore."

I said, "But, honey, you *are* my baby."

Little did she know that I had cried every morning for

those two weeks. I couldn't imagine my "baby" being old enough to be in school — to be away from me!

And she said, "I am *not* your baby; I'm in school now. You have Jason, and you can call him 'baby,' but please do not call me 'baby.'"

She was very serious. She said, "You can do it at home just between you and me, but not in front of my friends."

"You Be Mama and Let Me Be God"

After she left for school that day, I really cried...and cried...and cried! Then, finally, I began to pray. The Lord so sweetly said to me, "You be Mama and let Me be God. I'll take care of her!"

Heaven and earth may pass away, but God and the Word are forever. Perhaps I can't always be there, but God can!

That's why we *must* put the Word of God in our children. God said that He would never leave them or forsake them. He'll be there for them.

We saw where the Bible promised the Word will lead our children. It will keep them, and it will talk with them. We must fill our children with the Word of God in every aspect of their life, so that no matter what they face in life, they will be obedient to God, even though we're not there to guide them ourself.

Little Ones Grasp Spiritual Things

It's important to begin teaching children the difference between their *heart* and their *head* at an early age, because their head will try to get them in trouble.

We would tell our children very early, "You know, baby, what talked to you *down here* and what talked to you *up here*?" — pointing to their heart and their head. They didn't always know how to respond with words I could understand, but I could see in their eyes that they knew what I was talking about.

When Jason was 27 months old, we were lying in bed one morning having devotions. As soon as we finished, Jason picked up a little book he wanted me to read to him.

Instead of handing me the book, he held it up as if he was going to throw it. He turned his little blue eyes at me, smiled, and asked, with the book still held high in the air, "Do you know what the Holy Ghost said to me?"

"No, I don't. What did He say?"

"Well," Jason said, "He told me to obey you, but my head said, 'Just throw the book.'"

I smiled at him and said, "So what are you going to do, Jason — obey what's down here in your tummy, or what's in your head?"

"Here, Mama," he said. "I'll be obedient." And he sweetly handed me the book.

That was the first time he had ever verbally recognized the difference between his heart and his head. So I really made "a big deal" out of how proud I was of his obedience.

How quickly our children learn!

You can see that even at an early age, our children can distinguish between right and wrong because of what we put into them. That's why it's important that we put the Word of God into them, and that their convictions are *based on the Bible.*

When you're not there to tell them "why," they will remember the Word and say to themselves, "*This* is why I shouldn't do that: the Bible says I shouldn't." Their knowledge of the Word will remain with them.

John 6:63 says that the Word of God is spirit. That's why we must begin explaining spiritual things to our little ones. Yes, they may live in a small body, but they are a spirit and I am a spirit. God is Spirit, and God says that His Word is spirit. So we must begin communicating the Word of God from birth — and even in the womb. Our children can understand spiritual things long before they can communicate these things back to us.

Several years ago, I read an article which stated that doctors finally said they believe children can see at birth. I thought, "Thank you." Every mother has always known that, but doctors told us the babies couldn't see.

I know that babies can not only *see*, but they can *understand* as well. They *can* understand!

Children Are Not Born Disciples

Isaiah 54:13 promises us, "And all thy children shall be taught of the Lord; and great shall be the peace of thy children."

The Amplified translation renders it, "And all your...children shall be disciples — taught of the Lord [and obedient to His will]; and great shall be the peace and undisturbed composure of your children."

Many Christian mothers and fathers know and quote this verse all the time over their children, and they think it's just wonderful. Sunday School teachers quote it all the time, too. "Oh, *great* is their peace and undisturbed composure..."

But quoting it so blithely isn't enough. *How many of us are willing to do what it says: TEACH our children to be disciples of the Lord?*

Our children's peace and composure are the *result* of their becoming disciples of the Lord Jesus Christ. *Children are not born disciples.* The word "disciple" simply means "a disciplined one," one who is disciplined.

Yes, great *can* be the peace and undisturbed composure of our children *when we make them disciplined ones*, and when we teach them of the Lord and make them obedient to His will. *Then* great is their peace and undisturbed composure. But not before!

We have the responsibility to teach our children about the Lord.

Daily Devotions for Children?

A minister's schedule is never the same two days in a

row. Our schedules were especially crazy right after Janae was born, and we felt justified in not having a devotional time in our home. We thought we just couldn't do it.

However, we would take every opportunity to train Janae in the ways of God and His Word, just as we do with Jason now. For example, if there was something she really wanted to do, but didn't think she could, we would say, "Janae, honey, the Bible says in Philippians 4:13 that 'I can do all things through Christ which strengthens me,' so you can do this if you want to, because Jesus will help you."

When she would wake up during the night, afraid, we'd say, "Janae, God hasn't given you a spirit of fear, but of power and love and a sound mind.' (2 Timothy 1:7.) And 'Greater is He that's in you than he that's in the world.' (1 John 4:4.) And if you resist the devil, he has to flee from you." (James 4:7.)

We must be careful to take every opportunity during the day or during the night — whenever — twenty-four hours a day — to teach our children and impart the Word of God into them.

We did this so consistently with Janae that we really felt justified in our hearts that a regular devotional time wasn't necessary. But the Lord spoke to our hearts about the importance of a daily devotional time. He particularly spoke to me, because I'd never had a devotional time growing up, and it had always been a struggle for me to have a daily devotional time with God, except in emergencies.

"Create That Desire Within Them"

The Lord said to me, "That verse in Proverbs 22:6 says, 'Train up a child in the way he should go; and when he is old, he will not depart from it.' If you will require of your children a daily devotional time now, and create that desire within them, when they get old, they'll never depart from it."

So we had to change. Now we have a devotional time daily with our children. Because they are four years apart, I have to sometimes separate them because they are at such different levels of development.

In the morning, we sit down together, have devotions, and pray for a few minutes. I usually don't read from the *King James Version* to them; I read either *The Living Bible* or the *New International Version*.

Children's devotional time shouldn't be too long. For young children, perhaps five to ten minutes. Give them one thought each day to feed and meditate on: perhaps one scripture, or one phrase, or one Bible principle, or one Bible hero, and so forth. Cause them to realize that this is important to their everyday life.

It's true that if we'll train up our children, we'll create that desire within them for God, and they'll never depart from it.

For my children, this is a fun thing to do. They don't think, "Oh, no —boredom time! It's time for devotions." They *love* the fact that when they get out of bed in the morning, they can run and get their little devotional books. They *love* the time we spend together having our devotions. It's a part of their life, and when they don't have it, you can tell it.

When we have to go out of town and cannot take our children, the one thing I tell our baby sitters is, "The most important thing to do for my kids all day long is lead their devotions when they get up in the morning."

We have found from reading books on human behavior that the most important times in a person's day is when he first gets up in the morning and just before he goes to bed at night. The experts say that we remember those two parts of our day more than any other part of the day.

That's why I have a devotional time with my children first thing in the morning. Then we pray together as a family just before our children go to bed every night.

Find out what you need to do for your children, and put it into action right away. Leading them in devotions sometime during your day does not need to take up a lot of your time. But you do need to instill God's Word into them until it becomes a part of their very life and nature.

Looking Well to the Ways of Your Household

Now let's return to Proverbs 31. I believe the key verse that describes this virtuous mother is verse 27, which says that "she looks well to the ways of her household."

We must require the same behavior at home that we expect from our children outside of the home. Until you're willing to demand changed behavior from them *at home*, you'll never see different behavior *in public*.

For most of us, it's not in the home setting where we get most frustrated with our children's behavior; it's in front of family, or friends, or church friends, or neighbors.

But at home we often put "blinders" over our eyes and say to ourselves, "You know, I really didn't *see* them do that. It doesn't matter. I'm just going to pretend they did not do that."

Or you have already dealt with that misbehavior five or six times that day, and you don't want to have to deal with it again; you want to forget it. But if you do, that will warp the minds of your children.

Why? Because inconsistency on the part of adults confuses children. They'll continue to do something wrong as long as they *think* they can get by with it. But when they find out that you're going to be *consistent* — that you're going to look well to the ways of your household and not allow them to misbehave — they'll get in line quickly.

This is an important aspect of child-rearing, and it goes from A to Z in their lives.

Well-Behaved Children

When Jason was about two weeks old, I had to take him to a ladies' meeting with me. We have our ladies' meetings in homes, and this wasn't a very big home. Another woman was speaking that day, so I felt everything would be all right;

I could take the baby along and I could handle him.

We ate together and then, just as this woman started to speak, Jason started to cry. And he cried and he cried. I had just fed him, so I knew he wasn't hungry. I took him into the hostess' bedroom, thinking I could get him settled down and return to the meeting. But he didn't settle down. He kept getting louder and louder and louder. I didn't know what to do!

It's bad enough for something like this to happen at home, but when everyone is there, your mind can't think straight, and you wonder, "What am I going to do with him?"

He was getting so loud, I knew the speaker was having a hard time being heard; he was almost drowning her out, yet she was in another room!

So I thought, "Well, I'll just take him outside, and surely I'll get him settled down out there." He had gotten really hot inside the house. Outside, he started cooling off. Then all of a sudden, it started raining.

We were outside a sliding glass door, so all the women could see me out there, dancing around with Jason in the rain, pleading, "Oh, Jason, please be quiet! Please be quiet." And he was screaming his head off.

Finally I just stopped. I said, "Lord, what is the problem? *Why* is he acting like this?" And I saw a little flashback of me at home, alone with the children. I was putting my makeup on and Jason was crying. I said, "It's all right," and I kept on doing my makeup. Another flashback: It was time for daddy to come home, and supper wasn't ready, so I just let Jason sit there and cry.

And the Lord said to me, "Until you require at home what you want outside the home, you're not going to get it."

You see, I had allowed Jason to do his own thing at home when it seemed like it didn't matter. But it *did* matter. I should have stopped doing whatever I was doing and given him my time when he needed it.

His screaming was frustrating and embarrassing to me in front of all the women in my church. I didn't know how to deal with him there because I hadn't dealt with him at home. That's the way it is: The manner in which we deal with situations at home will affect our children outside the home.

Remember: Home is the key!

The Undisciplined Child

Proverbs 29:15 *(Amplified)* says, "...a child left undisciplined brings his mother to shame" — frustrated, embarrassed.

We were at a public swimming pool several years ago, and a woman brought her 3- or 4-year-old son in. He was screaming, kicking, and crying. She was trying to get her things laid out beside the pool, and he was messing them up.

There was another woman there with her. They both had puzzled expressions. They looked at him like, "What do we do with him?" Then he started running down the side of the pool, grabbing people's things and throwing them in the water!

The mother was so frustrated and embarrassed; she was running after her child, but he was going so fast, she couldn't catch him. As she ran, she was apologizing to all these people. She was saying, "I'm sorry; he never acts like this at home. I've never seen him do *this* before!"

I felt sorry for her. I wanted to help her, but I didn't know her. Everyone was staring at the child, and when he headed their way, they grabbed their belongings.

I wanted to stop the mother and say, "Listen, he *is* doing these same things at home. He's doing these things *somewhere*. But because it didn't matter at home, because no one else could see it, you didn't do anything about it."

Whatever you want your children to do in front of other people, make them do it in front of you when it *seems* like it doesn't matter. That's hard to do at home, when no one is there but you, and no one sees it but you.

In fact, I've had these words cross my mind sometimes: "Just pretend it didn't happen. Turn your back, and they'll never know you saw it." Often our minds want to tell us it's not worth it. Our minds will say, "You don't have time to deal with this. You're in a hurry."

Of course, when our children repeat their bad behavior in front of others, you can't wait to get home to deal with them! You can't blame them, however; you have to blame yourself for not handling it when it first manifested at home.

If you're not willing to discipline your children at home, please don't discipline them in front of other people.

"Hide the Breakables; We're Coming Over"

Most child training books recommend, "Child-proof your home. Get rid of everything you don't want broken until your child gets to be 4 or 5 years old." When I read that, I think, "And so what do you do when you go to *grandma's* house?"

We're pastors. We have to take our children with us to other people's homes. What am I supposed to do? Call the people first and say, "My brats and I are coming over. Would you please put your breakable things up"? (Sometimes I wish people would call me and say that to me!)

I do agree that we need to child-proof kitchens, bathrooms, laundry rooms, and wherever else children can find harmful chemicals. That is important. Don't be foolish and endanger your children's lives.

What I mean is, you don't need to hide all your pretty things and breakable objects. If you do, when the child *does* see pretty things at someone else's house, he's going to go nuts.

Then what will happen to you? You'll be frustrated and embarrassed. You'll have to say, "I'm sorry he broke it. How much was it? I'll try to pay you back." And they'll say, "Well, it was my great-grandmother's." There are things in life that are not replaceable.

So I can tell you, I've trained my children, *contrary* to what is commonly recommended. I've left pretty things around the house and taught my children not to touch them. And now I can take my little children wherever I want to and not get frustrated, embarrassed, or in fear.

For example, during a two-hour delay at the Dallas airport, Jason ran into a shop, got down on his knees, and watched some expensive mechanical toys that were making wonderful noises as they spun around a table.

As I caught up with him, the clerk said to me, "Get him out of here!" I said, "He is fine. He won't bother those things." She said, "I said, get him out of here!"

All he wanted to do was *see* these devices, so I picked him up and took him over to them. I picked one up and let him examine it. The clerk was really aggravated with me by then.

But children have a sense of curiosity within them that needs to be developed — a sense of seeing, of touching, of smelling. These things need to be developed within them. If we deprive them of this sensory knowledge, it will hinder their development.

What we can do is forbid them to touch things until we allow it under our supervision. With little children, you have to watch their eyes to see what they're looking at. That's all Jason wanted in that shop; he wanted to see that toy so badly. Once he had *seen* it, he was as happy as he could be.

I put him down and we left the store. The clerk probably cheered. Most people expect children to be destructive. That's why they yell, "Get them out of here. They're going to break something!"

We do need to be careful that we don't allow children to destroy other people's things. I trained my children at home how to handle nice things *with my supervision*.

When Janae was growing up, we didn't have too much to set around as decorations, but I was careful that when she went into other people's homes, she touched their pretty things only with my assistance and supervision. It's not too difficult to do this, but you do have to be consistent.

Now we can take our children into any store or home we want without holding onto both of their hands and praying they won't touch something. It makes your life peaceful when you do this.

Respect for Elders

Another thing we've done is to require our children to say to us, "Yes, ma'am" and "No, ma'am" and "Yes, sir" and "No, sir." Most of the time, Jason will say, "Yes, ma'am" and "No, ma'am." If he doesn't, I just ask him the question again. Sometimes I have to ask it four or five times. Then, all of a sudden, it "clicks," and he'll say, "Yes, ma'am."

We're doing this because we want to teach our children to treat other people with respect. Then, when they're around an elderly person, we don't have to prompt them by saying, "Say, '*Yes*, '*ma'am*,' honey." They've already learned this at home.

Don't wait until your children get to school and think the schoolteacher will teach them these things. It's our job. Whatever we want our children to be, we need to teach them to be that at home.

I'm using these situations from my family simply as principles or methods of training children to be a success. Your children may face entirely different situations than mine face.

Every one of you can think of behavior you've seen outside your own home that made you wonder, "Why is my child doing this?" When I see my children do or say things I don't like, I check up at home first. I realize that I need to change some things that I am doing at home. *Children will do what you say when they're young, but they'll do what you do when they're grown!*

There is no use trying to blame a schoolteacher or someone else; I blame myself, because I'm the one my children are around the most, and I'm the one who is responsible to train them.

Anytime my husband and I see behavior in our children that we don't like, we look at each other and say, "Well, one of us is doing it."

Of course, children do pick up little habits from other children, but these habits usually are temporary. Behavior that lasts and lasts and lasts is probably going on in your home, and you need to make the necessary adjustments.

"Things To Come"

Most of the time, we, as parents, know the situation or circumstance we are about to take our children into.

One of our responsibilities is to instruct our children. John 16:13 says one purpose or reason the Holy Spirit was sent was to show us things to come. Why? So we would know how to respond!

Whenever I'm taking my children somewhere, I talk to them and let them know what I expect from them.

For instance, on the way to church, I remind them that I want them to sit quietly. Going to someone's home, I remind them to play sweetly and share. Going into a store, I remind them to ask me to show them things.

My reminders are said in an attitude of, "It's easy. You can do it," not, "You little brat, you'd better obey me this time!"

Too often, our children disappoint us around others because they never knew what we expected of them! Take the time — only a minute or so — and let them know how you expect them to act! Prepare them by conveying what you expect as well as the circumstances they'll be facing, and also the people who will be present.

Prayer and Works

We heard one minister say, "Pray like it's all up to God and work like it's all up to you!"

Our responsibilities in raising children are tremendous,

but God wants to help!

Jeremiah 33:3 says, "Call unto me, and I will answer thee, and shew thee great and mighty things, which thou knowest not."

It didn't take me long to realize that as a parent, there were a lot of things I "knew not"! I needed God to tell me things and show me things. I needed His help!

As different situations and circumstances arise in my children's life, I look to God and ask Him to show me how to encourage them, and what to say to them. Involve God in your parenting role. He knows best!

Children need the prayers of their parents. Who is going to pray for them if you don't?

Pray the Word of God over your children. Cover and surround them with your prayers. Don't wait until problems arise to pray, but pray for them every day, and problems won't seem nearly so big!

Take your children up in your arms, on your lap, or pull them up next to you and pray for them. If this is done on a regular basis, it won't seem awkward or strange to pray when there are problems.

Make prayer for your children a part of your daily life. Here is a prayer guide we pray for our children. This is by no means all you can pray for them. As you pray this, the Lord will add various things.

The Psalmist said, "Give ear to my words, O Lord, consider my meditation" (Psalm 5:1). As you pray this, you will find yourself being reminded of God's promises and your responsibility. (References taken from The Amplified Bible.)

Lamentations 2:19 — Father, in Jesus' Name, I arise and cry out in the beginning watches and pour out my heart to You and lift up my hands to You for the life of my children.

Psalm 72:15 — May I give myself to pray for _____ continually and praise _____ daily.

Deuteronomy 6:5 — I pray that _____ will love You,

O God, with all _____ heart, all of _____ soul, and all _____ might.

    Psalm 40:8 — That _____ would forever delight to do your will.

    Ephesians 6:1 — That _____ would honor and obey us and it will be well with _____, and _____ will live a long life on this earth.

    Third John 2; Psalm 91:7 — I thank You, Lord, for divine health in my family, and though a thousand may fall at _____ side and ten thousand at _____ right hand, it will not come near _____.

    Psalm 91:11 — Thank You, Father that You have given your angels charge over _____ to accompany and defend and preserve _____ in all _____ ways of obedience and service.

    Ephesians 4:32 — I pray that _____ would be kind to others, tender-hearted (soft, delicate, considerate and compassionate), quick to forgive those who may wrong _____.

    Ephesians 5:1,2 — That _____ would always walk in love and follow after You.

    John 14:21 — Because _____ loves You, _____ will obey You, and You will manifest Yourself to _____.

    Psalm 16:11 — Because _____ is in your presence, there is fullness of joy in _____ life.

    First Peter 2:2 — Give _____ a desire and hunger for your Word, that _____ would grow by the Word.

    Romans 12:10 — That _____ would be kindly affectioned to others, preferring others above _____self.

    Psalm 112:2 — Thank you that my seed is mighty upon this earth.

    Proverbs 3:16,17 — That length of days is _____, riches and honor and wealth are in _____ house, _____ ways are ways of pleasantness, and all _____ paths are peace.

Isaiah 54:13 — For my child is a disciplined one, taught of the Lord and obedient to His will, and great is _____ peace and undisturbed composure!

Colossians 3:15; Philippians 4:7 — For the peace of God rules in _____ heart and guards _____ heart and mind through Christ Jesus.

Proverbs 6:22 — The Word of God will lead _____, the Word will keep _____, and the Word will talk with _____.

Second Corinthians 6:14 — I pray now, Father for _____ friends throughout _____ life, and for _____ mate that _____ would never be unequally yoked with anyone who is inconsistent with the faith.

Jeremiah 33:3 — I call unto You, Lord, and ask You to help me be a supernatural parent; show me great and mighty things concerning _____, that I may not know of.

John 16:13; Proverbs 31:25 — Show me things, Holy Spirit, that are to come concerning _____ life, that I might readily prepare _____ for the future.

Psalm 127:3 — I love You, Father, and I thank You for blessing me with wonderful children.

Matthew 6:13 — All the glory and praise and honor be unto You forever and ever... In Jesus' Name, AMEN!

Singing and Making Melody

Sing with your children! God said in Zephaniah 3:17 that He will rejoice over us with joy; He will joy over us with singing!

Something wonderful happens with song. Bring melody into your home! Singing can uplift the atmosphere of your home and the attitude of your family.

One time Jason said to me, "Nobody likes me! I'm just a nobody." Of course, I tried to encourage him.

That Sunday in Sunday School, his lesson was on "God Cares." When he came home with his papers, across the top it said, "God cares for *Jason*." So I began singing a little song:

God cares for Jason;

God cares for Jason;

God cares;

God cares;

God cares for Jason!

How simple a song! I just made up the tune. But it sure changed Jason. He began to sing it. Then he sang it to me and to Janae!

Song has a way of getting inside of us. It changes our thoughts and attitudes.

Create Your Atmosphere

We can create the atmosphere of our home.

The words we speak, the prayers we pray, and the songs we sing create the atmosphere of our home.

Make your house a haven your family enjoys coming home to.

People often comment that our home is so "peaceful." What makes it that way? The decor? The lack of clutter? No! We do!

The words we speak to one another set the atmosphere. Praying in your home for your children and with your children sets the atmosphere.

When things are going great — or when things aren't so great — sing a song!

"Anyway, Where Does God Live?"

"Just where is God? Does He live in heaven? Does He live at church? Where is He?"

These are valid questions of a child. How can you teach them that He's where they are? You can bring the presence of God into your home!

Isn't it wonderful to "feel" God at church? Well, we

need to give our children the privilege of "feeling" God at home!

Through all the things we've talked about — devotions, prayer, and singing together — we allow the Lord to move on us and in us — right in our own home with our own children.

In our times together like this, I've seen my children ask Jesus into their hearts. I've seen them cry for joy in His presence. I've seen them praise the Lord with their whole heart. What a privilege!

"Where does God live?" they ask. "Christ *in* you, the hope of glory" (Colossians 1:27). He is in them. He is where they are!

Conclusion

Our prayer for you is that God's Word inspires you to be the best parent possible. The Lord is your partner, and He's entrusted the next generation to us.

> **We will not hide God's will from our children, shewing to the generation to come the praises of the Lord, and His strength, and His wonderful works, that He hath done.**

> **For he...commanded our fathers, that they should make them known to their children:**

> **That the generation to come might know them, even the children which should be born; who should arise and declare them to their children.**

> **Psalm 78:4-6**

We are fulfilling this passage of scripture by arising and declaring God's will, His ways and love to our children. We are training our offspring this way, "...that they might set their hope in God, and not forget the works of God, but keep his commandments: And might not be as their fathers, a stubborn and rebellious generation..." (Psalm 78:7,8).

Don't Be Overwhelmed!

As you've read through the pages of this book, I'm sure the thought crossed your mind, "There is so much to do; there are so many areas I've missed it in, so many attitudes, words, and actions I need to change."

Don't be overwhelmed by the information. Begin today incorporating *one* aspect of the teaching. Ask the Lord to help you! Then as you daily make the effort to enact what you've learned, the Holy Spirit will bring other things you read to your remembrance.

We are on your side. We want you to be the most loving and effective parents you can be for your children's sake. You are not alone. Our prayers are with you. "If God be for us, who can be against us" (Romans 8:31).

Prophecy

Who can tell what the children shall do —
What steps will they take?
What deeds will they do?
Will they grow up to be strong?
Or will they fall to sin's allure?
Will they walk in righteous obedience?
Will their hearts stay clean and pure?

There are some who walk in wisdom,
For they see the great resource.
For these little ones who are raised in victory
Shall soon become a mighty force.
They'll grow up strong and be secure.
Not accepting defeat, their faith shall endure.
They'll laugh at sin
And all manner of disease.
And in the places that they walk
Sin's dominion will surely cease,
For they've been nurtured on the bread
So pure and true.

Satan himself shall tremble and say,
"Is there anything these children can't do?
They don't know how to be hungry.
They don't know how to be sick.

They don't know how to be defeated,
Or fall prey to my tricks.
Who filled these children with words of power?
Who instructed them in might?
I've not been faced with these before,
For these were trained up right!"

Then God shall laugh at the enemy,
For His little army has done well.
They've taken dominion over all the earth,
And run the devil back to hell.

— A prophetic poem delivered by Willie George
  at Kenneth Hagin's Campmeeting.